RISING HIGHER

Discovering Your Spiritual Gift DNA
- A Roadmap to Your Purpose

To contact
admin@erikalarsson.com

Erika Larsson

AUTHOR OF WINNING IN BUSINESS, AND LIVE OUT LOUD

You can find information on Erika Larsson's training seminars, speaking, video blog, and books at:

www.ErikaLarsson.com
admin@ErikaLarsson.com

Cover Design by Ann Crary of www.SeeItPrinted.com
Book Layout by Ann Crary of www.SeeItPrinted.com
Edited by Judy & Keith Hook, and Katherine Sciarrotta

DEDICATION

I dedicate this book:

To my daughter, Terrianne, who enthusiastically provides support for all I do in life. You mean the world to me.

To my mother, Goldie, for inviting me to church to hear a visiting evangelist speak in June 1972. It was at this life-changing event that I accepted Jesus Christ as my Lord and Savior. I'll forever be grateful to you, mom.

To my father, Gunnar, who is now with the Lord, for mentoring me in God's Word, and for his unwavering faith, and spiritual guidance. Without his support, I would not have the same love relationship with Jesus that I now have. I'm grateful that we will have a joyful reunion in heaven one day.

You have all contributed to who I am today, and for that I love you.

ACKNOWLEDGMENTS

My daughter, Terrianne, who speaks encouragement and hope into my life by telling me that the work I do, training others to know who they are in Christ Jesus, is what I'm meant to do.

My gratitude goes out to everyone who has contributed to the success of my book by editing, providing artwork, doing the book layout, and getting it to press.

I'm thankful for you, my reader for picking up this book. I'm thrilled that you want to learn about your gifting, and the plans God has for you.

Most importantly, a big thank you to God for putting passion in my heart to share the message of spiritual gifts, and how necessary they are for people to live a purposeful, joyful and fulfilling life. I am grateful to God for gifting me to encourage, inspire, motivate and lead. Apart from Him, I can do nothing!

Contents

←add scripture references to powr pts.

PART I

Introduction and Erika's Story

"The thing that is really hard, and really amazing, is giving up on being perfect and beginning the work of becoming yourself."
Anna Quindlen

INTRODUCTION

I first learned about the different personality styles in my late 20's. It had a profound, and positive effect on my personal and professional life. I learned why people behave and relate the way they do, and how to communicate and connect with them in meaningful ways. As well, I learned what the different style's preferences, values, needs, and stressors are, which helped me be effective in my interactions with others. I also discovered the correlation between personality styles and spiritual gifts, which have proven to be quite accurate.

I was raised going to church, but sadly, it wasn't until I was well into my adult years, that I learned about spiritual gifts. A mega-church I attended, ran an evening class for those who wanted to identify their gifting. At the end, we received a brief description of each gift, but there was no call to action to use them. I surveyed my church-attending friends who didn't attend and was surprised to learn that very few knew what their gifts were, and those who had identified them had either forgotten what they were or had never intentionally used them. This puzzled me. Why would God devote several chapters in the Bible to discussing the value of spiritual gifts; yet churches weren't encouraging its members to use them?

A few years later, another church I attended taught a class on spiritual gifts but only taught on nine out of the twenty-six gifts (this seems to be standard practice in today's churches). They encouraged people to get involved in the church and had a list of places within the church where the nine gifts could be used to serve. My gift profile did not include any of the nine gifts discussed, inferring there was no role in the church body for me. I felt disappointed and knew this was wrong.

After doing an in-depth Biblical study of spiritual gifts, I realized the importance God places on them for the health of the church body. According to the Bible, we are to use our gifting to share God's love and redeeming power with the world, yet few gifts are utilized in today's modern church. According to 1 Corinthians 12:12-27, which I highly recommend reading in its entirety, there is one church body with many parts (every believer is a part), and all parts have equal value. There is no hierarchy, no part (or gift) is more superior to another. Like a human body, each part (or gift) has a specific function that is necessary to the body as a whole. Take any part out of the equation, and the whole body becomes less powerful.

Spiritual gifts are not given for our benefit or self-advancement. God gave them to each believer for serving, and for enhancing the spiritual growth of the Body of Believers.

Unfortunately, today there are many churches with a hierarchical system of command; meaning most of its members have no part in the overall function of the church, other than to fill a pew and perhaps tithe. Sadly, this suits most people that attend a present-day church. The functions are run by a few elect decision makers, which means that the body is not as effective as it can be. To get a clear picture of what this means, imagine our overall physical body could only use our head, left hand, right foot, and one eye to perform all duties. We'd quickly learn that without the other body parts we accomplish far less than if the whole body functioned completely.

The commission of the church is to go and make disciples of every nation. To do this well, the body needs to be healthy, and it needs to have all its members participating and doing their part. The lack of spiritual gifts being taught or used in present-day churches significantly contributes to the lack of attendance and the church body's health. People need to feel like they have a valuable role and know that this is how God wired us.

I'm passionate about helping present-day churches increase their outreach and attendance by helping to wake Christians up to their gifting and how powerful and valuable they are in Christ Jesus. Before we were in our mother's womb, God had a plan for each and every one of us (Jeremiah 1:5), and it's a good plan! God has gifted us with everything we need for our journey as we serve Him. He loves us and wants us to be a conduit that He flows through to accomplish His work. He rewards those who are obedient with joy, peace, creativity, and fulfillment – God wouldn't have it any other way. He desires to have a relationship with us; and as our Father, He wants to bless us.

Gifts hold the key to understanding ourselves; why we think and act the way we do, how we relate to people and circumstances, and why we are energized and joyful when we perform specific tasks. Gifts are given to us by God, so we can be a useful servant; there is no higher calling.

Prepare to start your authentic journey, doing what God created you to do. Enjoy the book!

ERIKA'S STORY

"Who Am I?" and, "Why am I here?" These are questions most of us ask ourselves at some point in our lives. I was in my late twenties when these questions started haunting me. Why did I feel like I didn't belong, or fit in? Why was I always trying to please everyone around me to no avail? Was I flawed?

My search for the meaning of life brought me to a seminar that taught me about four personality styles. I remember feeling a great sense of relief there because, for the first time, I related and felt like I belonged, I felt normal. It was freeing to finally know that I was okay with the way I was and that there were even others similar to me.

I was raised in a family with both parents and three siblings. None shared my dominant personality traits, which meant I was completely different than anyone in my family. My parents did the best they could with what they knew, like all parents do; but, they were always trying to shape me into their image, like trying to fit a round peg into a square hole. It didn't feel good. I lost my identity and self-esteem along the way and became the "pleaser" in order to be loved and accepted.

I have vivid memories of my early childhood. At age three, I was already an entertainer. My family attended church regularly, and Sunday School was part of my life from birth. When visitors came, I would get my little stool and whatever book or magazine I could lay hands on, became my Bible. I would always preach from the book of Matthew. Possibly I had heard of it mentioned at church. My preaching was made up of whatever thoughts entered my three-year-old mind and company loved the entertainment, which was good for me. Later in life, I discovered that my spiritual gift DNA was already present at the tender age of three. I had quite the creative imagination and would use the silver trim located at the bottom of our white ceramic stove as my piano. Everyone would sing Jesus loves me or listen to my made-up songs. I loved their attention and the accolades and later discovered that my Promoter personality style loves to be on stage entertaining.

My mother's best friend, Solveig, played guitar at church. That, plus the way she dressed in beautiful dresses, captured my attention. I wanted to be just like her and was elated when I discovered a badminton racket that would serve as my guitar. This racket became a piece of me. So much so, that my mother sewed me a guitar case for it. Even though it had a white background with blue checks and red roses all over it; to me, it was a beauty!

I convinced my parents that I needed to play my guitar in church next to Solveig. I vividly remember the morning they agreed to let me bring my guitar to church. I proudly went to the front with my brightly colored case in hand and sat next to my mom's friend. I observed as she opened her guitar case and how she sat, spreading the full skirt of her dress on the bench before lifting her guitar to her lap. I copied her every move. Removing my badminton racket from my case, I proudly sat next to her. I played my badminton racket with gusto and sang my heart out! I'm sure God smiled down on my three-year-old heart that day. In the Bible we are constantly told to "be like little children," and I believe I know why. They are innocent and pure in their worship and beliefs.

I loved playing with friends and using my imagination. I was a little leader, always creating something fun and imaginative to do, inspiring others to partake in whatever I imagined.

By nature, my mom was a rule maker and everything was scheduled. She kept a tidy house and meals were served three times a day at the same time each day. She took pride in treating all her children the same. Mother insisted that her rules and routines be kept, which was opposite of the freedom and fun that my Promoter personality style craved.

My father, on the other hand, was fun and liked to play with us; tickling us, or doing outdoor activities with us, tucking us into bed at night with a firm hug. It was easier for me to bond with my father than my mother. But it wasn't until I learned about the four personality styles that I began to understand why.

With all the structure, after the age of four, I became painfully shy. My siblings and I had lots of rules to follow and I was constantly told to sit still, talk less, mind my manners, follow orders, and be quiet. We were taught as children, we should be seen and not heard; and our thoughts and feelings took low priority. My self-expression and self-esteem diminished in this environment.

School became my refuge; a safe place to express a little of what was left of my personality. I was good at following rules by this time, but always had report cards that said I talked too much in class. As a teenager, sports became my favorite outlet for my competitive nature. Physical education and art classes are what kept me in school the last two years of high school. I was an honor roll student; but I was often bored and spent endless time in the principal's office for skipping class. Rebellion had set in.

My need for freedom had brought me to the workforce at age thirteen. My immigrant family didn't have much money, so working part-time provided the cash to buy the latest fashion and do things I desired to do. A few days after my sixteenth birthday, I moved out from my parent's home and was on my own. I never lived under their roof or rules again. Moving out was my desperate fight to have the freedom I ached for.

Can you relate to my story in any area? Were you a child that heard negative comments about who you were during your upbringing? Did your parents or guardians try to make you into a blueprint of them? These parental behaviors often leave a child with low self-esteem, pain, and confusion about who they are. Often people with such an upbringing never find their road to recovery and are left living a life that is void of power, freedom, self-esteem, and self-expression. It seems difficult for these people to see what they are naturally gifted and talented at doing, having had it squashed for years. Luckily, I found my way and now I teach others to find theirs as well.

My passion is to help people discover the truth of who they are and were created to be. This knowledge will change your life, as it did mine, I promise. Knowing the four personality styles is a good start to the journey of self-discovery; and, you will see how the spiritual gifts fit perfectly into the four personality categories.

As mentioned earlier, most parents do the best they can with what they know. My parents loved us unconditionally. However, like many parents, they knew nothing about personality styles, or the associated behaviors, values, and needs of each style. Having this knowledge is so valuable. It will enhance your life and your relationships. Knowing the four personality styles will definitely help you be a better parent, life partner and friend.

In this book, I have provided all the resources required to help you identify your personality style, your spiritual gifting, and your purpose, which will help answer these questions, "Who am I?" and, "Why am I here?" My goal is to point you towards your best life, using your innate gifting to live a life of passion and purpose while falling deeply in love with the God who uniquely created you.

Get ready to have a joyous, energized, and fulfilling life, enjoying all of God's promises and blessings! You were created for greatness; it's time to claim what's been gifted to you for His glory!

PART II

God Has the Plan

"Commit to the LORD whatever you do,
and your plans will succeed."
Proverbs 16:3

Chapter 1

It All Starts with God!

BEFORE YOU WERE BORN GOD KNEW YOU

God chose you and set you apart before you were born. He already had the plan and purpose for your life and gifted you accordingly.

"Before I formed you in the womb I knew you, before you were born I set you apart." (Jeremiah 1:5)

"In Him we were also chosen, having been predestined according to the plan of Him who works out everything in conformity with the purpose of His will." (Ephesians 1:11)

"I am your Creator. You were in My care even before you were born." (Isaiah 44:2a CEV)

YOU ARE NOT AN ACCIDENT

God Chose to Create You

Mother Nature did not make you, nor were you just a biological combination of your parents' sexual passion. You were not an accident. You were created by the Almighty Creator who breathed life into you. You were made in God's image. He created you to do good works which He prepared in advance.

"So God created mankind in His own image, in the image of God He created them; male and female He created them. God saw all that He had made, and it was very good." (Genesis 1:27 & 31)

"For we are God's workmanship, created in Christ Jesus to do good works, which God prepared in advance for us to do." (Ephesians 2:10)

GOD CHOSE YOUR PARENTS

God Carefully Knit You Together in Your Mother's Womb

When you were merely a tiny embryo, God began to shape you and form you. He made you unique, a one-of-a-kind original. Because He already knew your purpose, He carefully knit into your DNA your gifting, your character traits, likes, dislikes, strengths, weaknesses, your perspective on life, and He was pleased.

"You made all the delicate, inner parts of my body and knit me together in my mother's womb. Thank You for making me so wonderfully complex! Your workmanship is marvelous—how well I know it. You watched me as I was being formed in utter seclusion, as I was woven together in the dark of the womb. You saw me before I was born. Every day of my life was recorded in Your book. Every moment was laid out before a single day had passed. How precious are Your thoughts about me, O God. They cannot be numbered! I can't even count them; they outnumber the grains of sand! And when I wake up, You are still with me!" (Psalm 139:13-18 NLT)

God created you with unique gifts and abilities that would help you serve others. And, He instilled passion in you to help you enjoy performing the things He had planned for you to do.

THE BODY, SOUL, AND SPIRIT OF MAN

You Are Made Up of Body, Soul, and Spirit

All human beings have a body that we reside in. We have a soul, which is our total self, and a spirit that lives eternally.

Body: Your physical being incorporates five senses (taste, sight, smell, hearing, touch). We make our bodies happy with essentials like grooming, exercise, clothing, food, and shelter.

Soul: Your mind, will, emotions and conscience are comprised of your likes, dislikes, character traits, and personality. We make our souls happy with relationships, material goods and activities we enjoy doing.

Spirit: The sphere of God-consciousness is the spiritual realm. It's the part that God communicates with and flows through. It's what allows us to have a relationship with God, where He gives us understanding, meaning, purpose, and enables us to love. We make our spirits happy with service to others, prayer, worship, reading and meditating on God's Word.

Feeding the body and soul first (the temporal things of life) leaves us dependent upon ourselves which often leads to emptiness and continued dissatisfaction.

Feeding our spirit first (the eternal) by reaching outside of ourselves to something much bigger, feeds the eternal which is the only thing that will satisfy us.

God intended that our body, soul, and spirit would be a vessel to contain Him, express Him, and function together to fulfill His purpose.

"May God Himself, the God of peace, sanctify you through and through. May your whole spirit, soul and body be kept blameless at the coming of our Lord Jesus Christ." (1 Thessalonians 5:23) + 24 "he will do it"
our part is to mortify ounselves + let the
holy spirit operate his power in us, while we
Ps 32:1-8, observe and are taught by his spirit,
living in us. In our own strength we interfere
and need a bridle because we have no natural
understanding.

CHAPTER 2

---✦---

WHAT GOD WANTS FOR YOU

God desires to give us a life of peace, joy, and fulfillment; free from worry. All this comes through Jesus, who is the answer to this life.

PEACE OF MIND AND HEART, AND OVERFLOWING JOY

"I am leaving you with a gift – peace of mind and heart. And the peace I give is a gift the world cannot give. So, don't be troubled or afraid." (John 14:27 NLT)

"I have loved you even as the Father has loved Me. Remain in My love. When you obey My commandments, you remain in My love, just as I obey My Father's commandments and remain in His love. I have told you these things so that you will be filled with My joy. Yes, your joy will overflow!" (John 15:9-11 NLT)

FULFILLMENT AND A WORRY-FREE LIFE

Unless we interfere with God's plan for our life, we will reach the highest form of fulfillment and joy available on earth. Because of sin, we will only achieve ultimate fulfillment and happiness when we reach heaven.

From the time God starts to form us in our mother's womb, He calls us by name, knows what we can do, what we'll be, and what will give us the greatest joy. God wants what is best for every person, but we have a choice, and often we choose to go our own path which lacks in the blessings He desires to give us. Jesus is the way, the truth, and the life – He is God's gift to mankind.

Do you worry? Jesus said, not to worry about food, shelter, clothing. And do not worry about tomorrow, for tomorrow will worry about itself, as stated in *Matthew 6:25-34,* a passage worth reading in its entirety. God promises in this passage *(verse 33)* that if we seek Him first, then all the things we need will be provided.

God loves us like a father. *Psalms 91* states that God is our refuge and fortress, He will protect us, and like a bird, He will cover us with His feathers, and under His wings, we will find safety from danger or trouble.

"Do not be anxious about anything, but in every situation, by prayer and petition, with thanksgiving, present your requests to God. And the peace of God, which transcends all understanding, will guard your hearts and your minds in Christ Jesus." (Philippians 4:6)

TRUST GOD - HE HAS THE PLAN

When we trust our lives to God, He will open doors that others cannot; He will counsel us, direct our path, and prosper us. With promises like these, why would we lean on our own understanding?

I encourage you to spend some time reading, reflecting and meditating on the following promises:

"Trust in the Lord with all your heart and lean not on your own understanding; in all your ways acknowledge Him, and He shall direct your paths." (Proverbs 3:5-6 NKJV)

"For I know the plans I have for you," declares the Lord, "plans to prosper you and not to harm you, plans to give you hope and a future." (Jeremiah 29:11)

"I will instruct you and teach you in the way you should go; I will counsel you with My eye upon you." (Psalm 32:8 ESV)

"Commit your work to the Lord, and your plans will be established." (Proverbs 16:3 ESV)

PART III

Understanding the
Four Personality Styles

"Always be yourself, express yourself,
have faith in yourself, do not go out and look for
a successful personality and duplicate it."
Bruce Lee

CHAPTER 3

---*---

HISTORY of
PERSONALITY TEMPERAMENTS

Mankind, in an attempt to fully understand human behavior, had categorized people into four main personality styles as far back as 370 BC, when Hippocrates created one of the very first systems recorded. Numerous personality systems exist today; designed by experts such as Jung, Meyers-Briggs, Keirsey, Lowry, Miscisin, and many others. They all share the same basic information but use different names for the four personality styles. I will spare you the details regarding the various systems, other than the one I designed called the "Live Out Loud Personality System™." This system uses names that are self-explanatory and easy to remember.

COMPARISON OF PERSONALITY TEMPERAMENT SYSTEMS

Live Out Loud Personality System™ Erika Larsson (the 2000's)	Supporter	Promoter	Planner	Thinker
Mary Miscisin (the 2000's)	Connector	Mover	Planner	Thinker
Don Lowry (the 1970's)	Blue	Orange	Gold	Green
David Keirsey (the 1970's)	Idealist NF	Artisan SP	Guardian SJ	Rational NT
Myers-Briggs (the 1950's)	ENFJ INFJ ENFP INFP	ESFP ISFP ESTP ISTP	ESTJ ISTJ ESFJ ISFJ	ENTJ INTJ ENTP INTP
Carl Jung (the 1920's)	Feeling	Intuition	Sensing	Thinking
Hippocrates (370 BC)	Yellow Bile	Blood	Black Bile	Phlegm

Chapter 4

---*---

Everyone is Uniquely Gifted

Everyone is unique and gifted! We are so complex that no one in the entire world is an exact duplicate of anyone else, not even identical twins. So, are we typecasting and putting people in a box by stating that there are only four personality styles? The reason we use this human behavior model is because for centuries it has been proven to be a simple, worthwhile method of identifying, and understanding mankind's behaviors.

We should always keep in mind that many variances come into play when we identify someone's personality style. Even though someone may have the same personality style as another and their style ranking scores may be identical; their similarities and differences, and how they respond to a situation may completely differ. People's behavior, is largely shaped by the way they were raised and the past experiences they have had. Both contribute to the person they become. Some are skilled at using their gifts more than others; some are introverted, while others are extroverted. All variables play a major role in what makes each of us a unique, one-of-a-kind individual.

Thinking that our personality style is superior to others is prideful. No style is better than another. We are all here for a purpose, and from birth have been gifted with natural abilities and talents. With ease we employ these gifts, experiencing creativity and joy when doing so. Our natural abilities continue to develop with use; eventually making us an expert in the areas we are gifted. Once we recognize our differences, we can work together, enrolling the gifts of others when we face a task that drains us - this is how powerful teams are built.

People are primarily dominant in one of the four styles, meaning that they have a natural way of behaving that is built into their DNA. We learn to differentiate each style by their unique gifts; how they process, behave, and function in the various scenarios of life. Being able to identify the most dominant characteristics helps us to begin the process of understanding ourselves and makes it easier to distinguish the similarities and differences of other styles as well. By learning what the four styles' attributes, needs, and stress inducers are, we begin to appreciate and accept their uniqueness, which is the first step to creating meaningful relationships.

The quickest way to discern a dominant gift is by how effortless the gift is performed. When a gift is in action, it is accompanied by a flow of energy and creativity. As a matter of fact, we could spend countless hours performing any dominant gift without tiring out.

Accessing this knowledge can help chart our course with confidence, and steer us towards doing what we were created to do. Understanding the differences and the contributions each style can make, is powerful information that will improve our personal effectiveness in all areas of life.

CHAPTER 5

———————✦———————

ARE YOU AN INTROVERT OR EXTROVERT?

According to renowned psychologist Carl Jung, credited as pioneering the terms "extroversion" and "introversion," there are two mutually exclusive attitudes, which children in their early years display with accuracy. Their preference for extroversion or introversion prevail throughout adulthood. The only time this may change is under extreme stress and unusual circumstances. The simplest way to understand the differences between extroverts and introverts, is to see whether someone generates and maintains their energy outwardly or inwardly. Extroverts are energized more by the external world and introverts are energized by their internal world.

The extrovert is most concerned with the world of objects, other people, and with how they impact the world. They are socially active, and most are well-informed about events taking place in their surroundings. They like to join groups, communities, and activities where they can easily interact with others. Introverts, on the other hand, prefer being by themselves. They enjoy alone time, with their thoughts and feelings, seeing the world in terms of how it connects to them. They think deeply and get energized and refreshed in quiet and solitude.

It is important to note that there are varying degrees of introversion and extroversion, depending on a person's state of mind, experiences, and phase of life. We all think, feel, sense, and experience the world in many different ways. Remember whether you are an extrovert or introvert, everyone is hardwired a certain way with characteristics that dictate how they gather their energy. We are all born with these preferences, and there is no right or wrong way to be.

It is much easier to determine the dominant personality style of an extrovert than it is an introvert, because extroverts share their dominant style with the world. Introverts use their dominant personality traits to process more internally, and typically communicate and behave in manners more indicative of their second style when interacting with the outside world.

With maturity, we can develop a flexible approach to our personality style, allowing us to choose the right attitude (extrovert/introvert) that fits in context to the situation or problem we are facing. This balance gives us freedom to be more of what we want to be, warding off a lot of unnecessary stress and wasted time.

The following characteristics are generally true for most extroverts:

EXTROVERTS

- Direct their focus and attention outwardly
- Are outgoing and energized by being with others
- Take in information through their five senses and focus on the here and now
- Focus on people and things
- Actively engage with their surroundings
- Speak and act readily without much reflection
- Like a flexible and spontaneous approach to life
- Naturally initiate conversations and interactions
- Like to participate in activities or situations that involve lots of people
- Have a breadth of interests and often have many friends
- Need to live and experience it to understand it

The following characteristics are generally true for most introverts:

INTROVERTS

- Direct their focus and attention inward
- Are energized by their inner world of ideas and impressions
- Have a hard time in large groups; too much interaction or small talk drains them
- Tend to make decisions based primarily on logic and objective analysis
- Recharge their batteries with solitude and solitary activities
- Focus on concepts and ideas
- Only participate verbally, when they have something to say
- Keep their social circle limited
- Prefer experiences with select individuals they are familiar or close to
- Tend to prefer depth of interest to quantity
- Need to understand it before they live it

CHAPTER 6

Identifying Your Personality Style

PERSONALITY STYLE WORD SORT

Rate how the words in the following columns describe your personality, by entering your scores in the boxes next to each word.

1 Point:	Least like me
2 Points:	Less like me
3 Points:	More like me
4 Points:	Most like me

To double check your personality style lineup, go to www.ErikaLarsson.com and take the free assessment.

Column A	Column B	Column C	Column D	
Peacemaker	Likes change	Prepared	Intellectual	
Accepts others	Bold and daring	Detail focused	Objective	
Supportive	Outgoing	On time	Likes to read	
Caring	High energy	Goal driven	Questioning	
Affectionate	Likes to talk	Traditional	Knowledgeable	
Likes helping	Risk-taker	Practical	Logical	
Patient	Quick to act	Organized	Problem solver	
Emotional	Playful and fun	Dependable	Likes technology	
Empathetic	Competitive	Responsible	Precise grammar	
Intuitive	Opportunistic	Likes routines	Innovative	
Good listener	Negotiator	Planner	Likes to fix things	
Spiritual	Straightforward	Hard working	Analytical	
Creative	Spontaneous	Loyal	Unemotional	
Nurturing	Freedom seeker	Follows rules	Private	
Avoids conflict	Multi-tasker	Efficient	Competent	
Total	**Total**	**Total**	**Total**	

Add up your scores for each column. Also, enter your totals in the Discovering Your Personality Style section below. Next, complete the Personality Style Ranking Lineup, using its directions.

DISCOVERING YOUR PERSONALITY STYLE

Insert your scores below for each column:

_____ Column A Score – SUPPORTER

_____ Column B Score – PROMOTER

_____ Column C Score – PLANNER

_____ Column D Score – THINKER

PERSONALITY STYLE RANKING LINEUP

Enter your personality style names in order of dominance below:

_____ highest score - Dominant Style

_____ 2nd highest score – Secondary Backup Style

_____ 3rd highest score – Third Style

_____ lowest score - Challenging Style

It is helpful to commit your style lineup to memory. We function mostly from our Dominant and Secondary Backup styles.

LIVE OUT LOUD PERSONALITY SYSTEM™ TERMS

Terms used to describe the four personality styles in this book are:

Supporter: Nurture and care for people

Promoter: Bring action and fun to the world

Planner: Work bees who get things done

Thinker: Change agents who improve the status quo

Every style is excellent in its own right. Our challenge is to recognize our differences, honoring each style's gifts and the contributions they make in life.

HOW YOUR PERSONALITY LINEUP AFFECTS YOUR ACTIONS

Dominant Style

Your primary, most dominant style is what guides and directs you through life's

32

experiences. The attributes of your dominant style are part of your DNA. You were born with these gifts; using them is as natural as breathing; they take little thought or effort to perform.

Secondary Backup Style

Your secondary backup or "go-to" personality style is the co-pilot that supports the actions of your most dominant style. Most people operate between their top two dominant styles most of the time. If you are an introvert, chances are you display this side of your personality to the public and use your dominant style inwardly in your alone time.

Third Style

You will access the traits of your third personality style when situations demand it. If your third style's score is close to your second, these traits will be more apparent, allowing you to access them with more strength.

Challenging Style

Your fourth rated style is often challenging. This is significant because the traits are the least natural to you. Chances are they are also the characteristics you least appreciate or understand, and therefore can cause you to criticize others who possess them. Your fourth personality style offers the most opportunity for growth.

DISCERNING YOUR PERSONALITY STYLE

Sorting out the perfect order of your personal characteristics may take some time. As you get more familiar with the traits for all four personality temperaments, you may discover more strength in a particular style than you had originally scored. Often traits of a parent were demanded of you. Therefore, you adapted these traits to survive in life, and they are now second nature, making it harder to evaluate your own natural gifts. The easiest way to reach clarity is to look at the gifts of each style, asking yourself if you are energized and happy when you carry them out or is it just a learned trait.

We all have characteristics from all four of the styles in varying amounts. Many personality experts agree, "Thinkers" are the most likely to report an equal spread of personality characteristics. Their keen ability to analyze helps them activate their brains to produce examples of circumstances in which they have used each trait. Once they continue their research and examine which traits energize them, and which they perform with less zest, they quickly determine that the majority of their preferences fit into the Thinker style. It's a typical process for the Thinker to question and to examine everything from all angles, but in the end, their analyses produce reliable results.

Understanding our own personality traits and what makes our style tick is a good start. Becoming proficient at identifying the styles of others comes with observation and practice. With a little training, you can skillfully discern the personality temperament of everyone you meet, with speed and accuracy, enhancing your relationships with those around you.

Everyone is gifted! Embracing our differences removes much of the stress in our day-to-day dealings with other styles.

PART IV

Decoding the Four Personality Styles

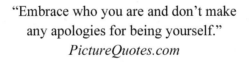

"Embrace who you are and don't make
any apologies for being yourself."
PictureQuotes.com

CHAPTER 7

---★---

MEET THE SUPPORTER PERSONALITY STYLE

Supporters are polite, friendly, and helpful. They love people and devote time to connecting with others; talking and listening, sharing feelings and profound truths. They are the least judgmental and most inclusive of all the personality styles, readily able to see different points of view, providing empathy and respect for individuality.

Their feelings can be easily hurt and when criticized, they have a hard time not taking it personally. They are emotional and wear their hearts on their sleeves, often crying with someone who is hurting or laughing with those who are happy. They will establish good eye contact, and make others feel cared for and comfortable.

Because they are perceptive and gifted with intuition, they read between the lines quickly, discerning false motives or intentions, even when no one is speaking. They instinctively know when a person is dishonest and when a person has unexpressed needs. Their perceptive nature helps them understand, accept and care for people more than any of the other personality styles and it's why they make excellent counselors.

Supporters are highly creative and have great imaginations. They are always seeking to understand the human race. Most are deeply spiritual and spend lots of time developing their inner self to gain understanding about their path and purpose in life.

They have to be careful not to become a real dumping ground for other people's problems. Giving too much empathy can cause them a sense of emotional heaviness, making it difficult for them to let go of sadness or concern they feel for others. If they are not careful, they will take on the problems of others as their own, which can result in depression. On the other hand, whenever a Supporter can provide useful insights, advice, and counseling they feel energized, fulfilled and happy. They do best by learning to create healthy boundaries with people.

Supporters are optimists. They see the good in everyone and will give people who hurt them chance after chance. Their support of others is unending. They are the wind beneath the wings of those leading the way and will assist in any way they can with necessary tasks. Coming to the aid of those who display a need, makes a Supporter feel fulfilled.

Emotional tension or the venting of hostility makes them extremely uncomfortable. Supporters are lovers, not fighters. They dislike conflict and will go to great lengths to foster harmony, cooperation, and togetherness. They prefer to walk away from a fight instead of engaging in it, both at home and in the workplace.

Supporters are nurturers and caregivers who possess a deep emotional attachment to their loved ones. Creating memories with their family and friends gives them a sense of purpose and great joy. Their loyalty and devotion to the people in their lives are second to none. They are the glue that holds relationships, organizations, and families together. Whatever they can do to make others feel good, they enjoy doing.

This quadrant of people is at peace, appreciating everything and everybody, and is contagiously enthusiastic. They like interacting with others and behave with honesty and integrity, always encouraging those who doubt themselves. You can ask them a question and expect to get a truthful answer.

They have lots of compassion for people and animals. Often, they will get involved in humanitarian or animal rescue projects and will come to the aid of anyone hurting. They can commonly be found helping individuals that are ill, disabled, disenfranchised, or otherwise in need. They help the helpless, adopt pets from the animal shelter and will support any cause that has affected them personally. They are tolerant, kind, and generous to those who display a need, be it in the physical, spiritual or emotional realm.

Supporters need meaning in their lives and feel special when others show appreciation for their authenticity and unique contribution. They focus on making a difference in the world, and their quest to do so is never-ending.

They prefer not to lead and enjoy being part of a team where they can inspire others and cheer for them. They are outwardly receptive and non-judgmental and sense the exact moment when people need nurturing, complimenting or validation. They are cooperative rather than competitive, and because they get along with others, they make excellent mediators.

Supporters have no need for power or control. Instead, they thoughtfully dedicate much of their time to helping others feel good about themselves. Helping others gives them a lot of peace and joy, and it's what fills them up. Hospitality is part of their DNA; they like cooking and entertaining, making it easy for guests to feel welcome in their home.

Most Supporters love nature and the outdoors. Nature is life to them, and they prefer to head out to the trails, mountains, and wilderness rather than spending time in the bustling city.

Supporters value personal growth and strive to balance mind, body, and emotions. To this end, they often populate self-help, bodywork, or human potential seminars, and often seek a career path in one of these areas. Supporters gravitate towards careers in alternative or complementary medicine such as homeopathy, massage, naturopathy, etc. Many opt to work as counselors, psychologists, nurses or in areas where they can help people, animals or the environment. Some express themselves in creative or fine arts careers like; music, drama, writing, painting, sculpting, graphic arts, or architecture to name a few. They are highly represented among journalists as they excel in both the written and spoken word.

Money is not as important to a Supporter as it is to the other three personality styles. It is seen as a tool to achieve ideals rather than a way to gain power, status, or win the admiration of other people. They are best described as "earthy," both in appearance and lifestyle. They are typically health conscious and seek alternative health advice outside the standard medical system, even if it means they have to pay for it themselves. Often, they garden and grow organic food. They like natural products, shampoos, cleaning supplies, etc., and may spend a lot of time at the health food store. They recycle, do their part to take care of the planet and get involved in causes that create positive change.

Supporters tend to collect keepsakes, mementos, souvenirs, and clothing that are meaningful to them. It is not unusual to discover their graduation, bridesmaid, or wedding dress tucked away in the closet or an item that a loved one gave them. They are very reluctant and unwilling to part with anything that has fond memories.

Because relationships mean more to them than things, they are often content with simple living arrangements, second-hand furniture, and décor. Extravagant meals, vacations or wardrobes are rarely high on their list of priorities.

Supporters wrote the book on romance and love giving affection, caring gestures, a hug or pat on the back. They may write poetry for their loved one and will always remember special occasions. They thrive when they feel loved and accepted and will bend backwards to ensure their relationships remain stable and intact. They have a phenomenal ability to love people unconditionally.

In their interactions with people, Supporters have the capacity to look beyond the immediate surface to see the real truth. They look for the good in people which often results in a romanticized view of others. They are known to stay in unhealthy relationships, hoping the person will eventually change for them. Their optimism and patience with people can also work in their favor, helping to create lasting relationships that thrive.

Supporters are very authentic and build relationships by sharing personal information from their heart. You can count on them being genuine, passionate and real in all their encounters. They generally have lots of friends, and most likely will keep their friends for life. They regard life as something to share, feel and experience with people. They desire to understand others and be understood.

Supporters have a sensitive nature and avoid mean, negative, or obnoxious people at all costs. They excel at motivating, encouraging and inspiring others to be their best. They are in the world to minimize conflict, be peacemakers, lovers, and supporters, giving hugs to all who need them, and a listening ear to a troubled heart. Their dedication is to make a difference in the world by helping others see their full potential.

A SUPPORTER'S GIFTS

All of us are here to use our gifts to make a contribution to the world. A dominant Supporter's gifts are a natural part of their DNA, making them effortless to use. Most of their gifts involve nurturing, creating, helping or supporting, which is their primary purpose in life.

They are passionate and represent love, harmony, and relationships. When Supporters are allowed to express their unique gifts, it contributes to their overall success and happiness.

- Fostering relationships
- Acknowledging others
- Caretaking
- Optimism
- Teaching and training
- Mercy and compassion
- Hospitality
- Empathy
- Nurturing
- Kind and considerate
- Encouraging
- Giving
- Sympathy
- Peacemaking
- Enthusiasm
- Helping and serving
- Supporting
- Affectionate - hugs
- Imagination and creativity
- Spiritual insights

- Intuition
- Listening
- Mentoring
- Communicating
- Patience and tolerance

- Motivating
- Recruiting
- Romance
- Sensitivity
- Connecting with others

JOYS

Supporters gain satisfaction, fulfillment and joy from the following:

- Affection and loving gestures
- Performing and fine arts
- Social acceptance
- Activities that promote unity and teamwork
- Using their imaginations
- Events that inspire them
- Personal relationship and friendships
- Plays and movies that are emotional

- Entertaining family and friends
- Being a positive influence in situations
- Nature and things pleasing to the eye
- Self-development, growth, and spirituality
- Love and romance
- Meaningful conversations
- Being creative
- Helping others

VALUES

Values are an inner guide that directs a Supporter's actions and gives their life purpose and meaning.

- Compassion
- Long-lasting friendships
- Peace and harmony
- Tolerance
- Honesty and integrity
- Intimacy and affection
- Nature
- Kindness

- Human potential – seeing the possibilities in others
- Self-actualization
- Spirituality
- Helping to meet the needs of others
- Sensitivity
- Creativity

- Communication, sharing, interaction
- Connection
- Patience

CORE VALUE: Relationships

NEEDS

Meeting a Supporter's needs is a sure way to gain their cooperation. Their comfort, health, happiness, and success, depends on satisfying these requirements through continued opportunities and experiences. When their needs are not satisfied, frustration and stress increase, which often leads to conflict; or worse, emotional or physical health problems.

- To be accepted, well-liked, understood, and included
- To live in peace and harmony
- Honest and sincere communication
- Freedom from control
- Appreciation and acknowledgment
- To be self-expressed, real, and personal; sharing thoughts and feelings
- To live a meaningful life of purpose; making a difference
- Conflict resolution
- To act in agreement with others to ensure no one is hurt, offended, or left out
- To affirm others and be affirmed
- Interaction with others
- To feel needed
- Love, romance, affection, and intimacy
- Relationships – family and friendships
- To cultivate potential in self and others
- To contribute; nurture, support, and care for the needs of others
- To use imagination and creativity
- To feel unique and special

STRESSORS

A Supporter's capacity to succeed in life is significantly diminished when they experience the following:

- Lying and cheating
- Controlling or aggressive people
- Insensitivity and insincerity
- Disharmony and conflict
- Isolation and being ignored
- Lack of communication
- Negative, arrogant, and rude people
- Lack of appreciation
- Having to say "No" to requests
- Being compared, talked about or criticized
- Lack of physical contact and affection
- Cruelty to people or animals
- Lack of individual expression
- Budgeting and financial planning
- People who lack warmth and caring
- Rushed timelines
- Being yelled at or spoken to in a harsh tone
- Tunnel vision without being open to new possibilities

REACTION TO STRESS

When Supporters are stressed out or overwhelmed, their personalities fade and their attributes quickly do an about-face and become their challenge. In this state, they often display attention-getting misbehavior and may even tell a lie to save face. They cry easily and appear depressed and withdrawn. Many will express their frustrations and emotions by yelling, screaming or using anger in hopes of gaining back control. All they need to return to their caring state and get back on track is a little reassurance, support, and love.

When experiencing low self-esteem or stress, they may behave in the following ways:

- Lie to "save face"
- Quit caring
- Play victim - wallows in self-pity
- Harbor resentment
- Disguise feelings with a false happy face
- Blame others, not taking accountability
- Dramatize events – using words like "always" or "never"
- Withdraw - spending time daydreaming and fantasizing
- Eat comfort food to soothe their wounded feelings
- Emotional outbursts – yelling, crying or exploding with anger
- Takes everything personally – become overly sensitive
- Control by giving the silent treatment
- Display rigid and uncooperative attitudes
- Become judgmental, or gossipy
- Become overly involved in helping others to avoid their own feelings
- Passive-aggressive
- Sabotage opportunities and relationships
- Social withdrawal from everyone close to them
- Serious mood, body language is unfriendly and closed off

TURN TO SUPPORTERS FOR:

Hospitality – Their door is always open, and they like having people drop in and stay for a chat, a meal or overnight. A Supporter's passion and focus are to make people feel welcomed, doing what it takes to help them feel safe, comfortable and included. No one will be alone when a Supporter is around. They make great greeters for any function. At work, they are great at helping newcomers get oriented.

Acceptance – Supporters value relationships and provide a tremendous amount of understanding, tolerance, patience, and mercy towards everyone they meet. Accepting, praising, encouraging and validating others, is as natural as breathing for Supporters.

MEdiATioN – They enjoy harmony and therefore exert effort to dispel any conflicts at home and work. They don't like to take sides in any dispute; instead, they will listen to everyone involved, fostering collaboration to reach an agreement, and ensure peace has returned. Their intuition guides them in the process, and because people sense that they are heard and cared about, they usually cooperate.

PERSONAl ANd SpiRiTuAl GROWTH – Most Supporters are very spiritual, and it's rare to meet an atheist. They claim to feel connected with a power greater than themselves and believe in God or a higher power. Supporters spend lots of time searching for the meaning and purpose of their existence and claim to find the answers in their chosen faith. Many attend church and most pray. They are proponents of personal growth and love the journey of learning, growing and living their full potential.

ENcouRAgEMENT ANd CHEERiNg Up – Supporters are cheerful and optimistic, gifted at seeing the best in both people and situations. They provide comfort and understanding and help others see the silver lining. Because they love to grow and learn from every circumstance life presents, they can encourage others to do the same. They use their caring, intuitive, and creative ways to lift spirits, in particular for those who feel downtrodden or sad. They are quick to give genuine compliments.

FRiENdsHip – Since Supporters value relationships above all else, they love connecting with others. As friends, they consistently listen, care, nurture, support, and encourage the people in their lives. They are super intuitive and know what to say and when to say it. They know how to comfort, and they know how to motivate people to be their best selves. You can count on a Supporter friend to be there for you when you need them.

SuppoRT – Supporters are excellent at supporting others to win. When you want a team cheerleader or someone to come alongside to lend a hand, involve a Supporter.

Guidance to Make Change – Supporters understand people better than anyone else and are experts at knowing how a change will impact the people involved. Because change often takes people out of their comfort zone, it's good to involve a Supporter as they understand what is needed to keep everyone calm and engaged, ensuring the transition from old to new will be smooth. They make great counselors as they have the ability to guide people to welcome change.

Teaching and Mentorship – Supporters are patient and love to guide others to reach their potential. They feel rewarded when others are inspired and motivated by what they teach. As a mentor, they know when to push their student and when to pull back, always keeping the pupil's needs in mind as they develop and learn. Their discernment about people allows them to adapt their teaching style, giving each student the attention, they need to learn best.

Teamwork – They are excellent team players and great followers. They are sensitive to the needs of others and are happy to roll up their sleeves and do what is necessary to reach the goal. They cheer everyone on and encourage team members to do their best, giving compliments that inspire and motivate them. They are masters at reading people and do what it takes to ensure they have a cohesive team.

Creativity and Imagination – If you want to brainstorm ideas and create training in the areas of service, morale building, team-building, communication or people skills, make sure you include Supporters. They have great imaginations that will help spark new original ideas as well as inspire everyone involved to contribute their innovative ideas. They are also very gifted at being craftsmen. Because of their artistic flair, many express themselves through writing, music, art, acting, decorating, building or making things. They are never short on ideas on how to make something beautiful.

Contribution to a Cause – Any cause or charitable organization that contributes to the well-being of people or animals will tug at the heart strings of Supporters. They love making a difference and don't mind volunteering their time or financial support to such a cause. They are quick to support organizations that provide humanitarian or animal rescue and help.

Event Design – Supporters love creating and are perfect candidates for developing an event, be it a wedding, a company party, or a family function. Their imagination and creative flair will help make the event a success. They take everyone's personality into account when they plan. A perfect combination would be to let the Supporter handle the parts of the function that requires creativity and have a Planner personality style, handle the logistical and budgetary details.

Help – Supporters love lending a hand, and when they can contribute to lightening the load, it energizes them. When asked to help, they will rarely say no. They are the wind beneath the wings of leaders. Supporters are the people who always show up to do work; no job is too small for them. When they contribute to others, they feel included, wanted and needed. They are the ones that help their friends move or bring a meal to someone who is sick.

Inspiration and Motivation – Supporters have a built-in gift of inspiring and motivating others. They especially love using these traits to help people reach their true potential in any area of life. In a work situation, they are a true asset to any team, as they know just what to say and do to inspire and motivate those around them.

Romance Ideas – No one understands love and romance better than Supporters. They could author several books on the topic. They love being in love, and showing romantic gestures is second nature. If you want to impress your romantic interest, take advice from a love pro, the Supporter.

Peacemaking – Harmony is super important to Supporters. They will help dispel any conflict to create a peaceful, harmonious atmosphere or relationship.

A Listening Ear – When you need to vent, a Supporter will be your confidante, providing active listening for as long as you need it. They are the least judgmental of all four personality styles and are gifted listeners, often without saying a word. They are patient, discerning and compassionate, and have the ability to understand and share the feelings of others without discrimination.

CHAPTER 8

---✳---

MEET THE PROMOTER PERSONALITY STYLE

Promoters are optimistic, have a light-hearted attitude towards life, a great sense of humor and are playful. It's a lot of fun to spend time with them. They love to laugh and remind us all not to take life too seriously. To them, life is to be enjoyed at every opportunity, viewing activities as a game to win. They are very independent and have lots of friends, interests, and hobbies.

They are extremely friendly, charming, and social, and have the ability to talk to anyone with ease, moving from one topic to another in conversation. Promoters tell the best jokes and keep the atmosphere happy, light, and entertained. If they don't laugh several times in a day, there is something wrong. They are great showmen who love sharing anecdotes and testimonials. They enjoy being the center of attention, not necessarily seeking it. However, they bask in it when it occurs.

Promoters possess natural childlike qualities and a certain innocence that others often find refreshing. They get over unpleasant setbacks quickly, and in a short time they forgive and move on. They are not afraid to let their inner child out to play and often come bouncing into a room announcing their presence. They bring energy, fun, and entertainment to all their social interactions. Most will tell you they don't want to grow up or grow old. They continue to be free spirits into their old age refusing to be confined or held back.

Their exceptional insight into people allows them to assess them instantly and mirror their body language and emotions to establish an immediate rapport. With their promoting nature, they promptly capture the attention of the public. They are very expressive and can entertain a crowd without effort, spontaneously sharing their entertaining stories. Promoters enjoy sharing interpersonal feelings and having deep conversations; your secrets are safe with them.

They catch on fast and act on and implement new ideas without missing a beat. Promoters don't like to practice; instead, they prefer to learn with a hands-on activity. They will spend hours perfecting an activity or skill, having a good time on the way to improvement. Because Promoters process information the moment they receive it, they find it difficult conversing with people who pause to think before they speak.

Promoters are happy people. They are active and outgoing. They can express themselves in a variety of ways which doesn't always appeal to every personality style; however, most people, in general, love their pleasant company.

They adapt well to new experiences and thrive on the unpredictable which is why the excitement of traveling is one of their favorite things to do – preferably first-class. They love to spend money and are by nature very generous and extravagant, giving expensive gifts to the people they care about, rarely paying attention to what is in their savings account.

Most personality styles don't like change, but Promoters love it and find it exhilarating. They lack fear and are risk-taking adventurers, who like movement, dancing, and physical activities. They like participating and living life to the fullest. Many pursue competitive sports or frequent a gym to expend some of their energy. If you want to bungee jump, skydive, ride a roller coaster or any other risky adventure, ask a Promoter to join you as they get a rush from these activities, and usually won't say no.

Like the Thinkers, Promoters love music, and many are highly skilled in this arena. Due to their artistic pursuits, most popular song artists, and entertainers are likely Promoter dominant personality styles. Some are so naturally talented in music that spending hours practicing like the Thinker style would is not necessary. Instead, they play when they feel the urge, taking pleasure in the countless hours they spend concentrating on their performance until they reach contentment. Their endurance level passes that of the other styles when they are focused. Because they naturally tend to focus on solutions, they can endure physical suffering, hardship, hunger, and fatigue in a way that other styles cannot. This stamina, along with their stubborn minds gets them through the most grueling of challenges.

Physical activity and motion help Promoters release emotional upsets, anger and bottled up energy, helping them to feel invigorated, bright and ready for action again. Promoters love the challenge of competing, and their goal is to place first in any activity. Their energy, self-esteem, and confidence are at an all-time high when they conquer and win a challenge.

Their antidote to avoid boredom is to keep busy and stay in action. Promoters constantly hunger for new experiences that will stimulate their five senses – new sights, smells, sounds, tastes, and touch. To gain their cooperation, tell them a story, use testimonials or concrete, practical examples when you talk to them.

Like the Thinkers, Promoters can also see the "big picture." They are visionaries, capable of seeing possibilities that others do not. Promoters are quick- thinking and accustomed to probing until they uncover new ideas. They are innovative when it comes to producing results, and they swiftly seize opportunities when they discover them.

Promoters dream "big" and have "big" goals, however, they rarely write them down. They are always making the right connections that will help bring their goals to fruition. They see the goal in their mind's eye and instead of creating detailed plans, prefer to figure things out as they go, changing course when needed. They like trying new things and are capable of creating whatever they think up. They are usually the ones that bring a fresh perspective or a new edge to an old idea to make it a hit. Because they read people well, they instinctively know what appeals to the masses, and this is what they seek to deliver.

Even though Promoters are not great at dealing with details, they have an excellent memory for detail and with ease can recall what occurred on a particular date, what someone was wearing at an event or describe every detail of the hotel room they stayed at last month. Promoters never forget the date or time of an upcoming event they want to attend; however, most struggle with remembering the mundane things like where they left their car keys, sunglasses, wallets, purses or what they were supposed to bring to the company barbecue.

They process information out loud and when they have a problem, they need to talk about it. More words come out of their mouths than any of the other personality styles. They have frankness of speech and can come across as blunt, speaking what is on their minds without giving much thought to how others may perceive what they say. They mean no harm; they are honest and dislike playing emotional games. What you see is what you get with a Promoter. If they offend anyone or hurt their feelings unintentionally, they apologize at once and make it right.

The great thing about a Promoter personality is that they don't sit and wallow in self-pity or hang onto hurt or anger. Instead, they let go quickly and move on to their next adventure. Even with life's setbacks and unfortunate events, Promoters typically adapt much faster than other personality styles, believing that everything happens for a reason and always works out in the end.

Many Promoters may underperform in academic settings; not due to a lack of ability, but to a lack of stimulation and challenge. Because they rapidly take in information, they get drained and 'check out' when forced to deal with abstractions or theories for too long. This explains why more Promoters than any other personality style, are apt to be diagnosed with ADD or ADHD. Because of their social prowess, they often distract other children in school rather than focus on their work. It is not uncommon for remarks to appear on their school report cards stating that they interrupt and talk too much in class. They are most productive in informal environments, especially when they can move about.

Promoters have a natural eye for beauty, style, and aesthetics and are concerned about keeping up their appearance. They are edgy, with a tasteful, flamboyant way of dressing and decorating their homes, and are never intimidated by loud colors or trendy styles. They keep up with current trends and fashions and are not afraid to try a new hair color or the latest fashion-forward hairstyle. They help to stimulate the economy because they buy what they like, without concern for cost. They are generous hosts, and their homes are always open to visitors.

They appreciate excellent food and know the best restaurants in town. They know where all the entertainment venues are and many like to frequent live theater. In their garage, you will find power tools, maybe a bicycle, a vintage or luxury sports car along with all types of sports and outdoor paraphernalia.

Promoters are the entrepreneurs of the world. They are unafraid of trying new things, blazing new trails with great zest and enthusiasm. They are swift on their feet, highly creative and multi-talented. They do well in a variety of careers, especially ones that involve action, movement, risk-taking, flexibility, creativity, and freedom of expression. They work well under pressure and can think on their feet. Careers in sports, fashion, hosting a TV show, acting, music, dance, sales or marketing are a sampling of what appeals to them. Others may work in construction, as firemen, pilots, negotiators, or mechanics, etc.

Even though they are restless and easily distracted, they can focus well when partaking in discussions and activities that are stimulating. Life is an adventure for Promoters. They like freedom and movement. They want to do what they want when they want, without having to answer to anyone or being confined by limitations and obligations. They are daredevils who release their excess energy through physical activities and action. Having challenges and the freedom to act is what makes them peek-performers.

A PROMOTER'S GIFTS

All of us are here to use our gifts to make a contribution to the world. A dominant Promoter's gifts are a natural part of their DNA, making them effortless to use. Most of their gifts involve action, adventure, promotion, and entertainment, which is their primary purpose in life.

They are energetic and represent fun, freedom, power, persuasion and swift action. When Promoters are allowed to express their unique gifts, it contributes to their overall success and happiness.

- Optimism and enthusiasm
- Adventurous nature
- Bravery and boldness
- Motivation
- Competitiveness
- Problem solving
- Creativity
- Resourcefulness
- Dealing with crisis
- Using tools
- Direct communicator
- Efficiency
- Quick to act
- Networking
- Flexibility
- Generosity
- Proficiency
- Humor and playfulness
- Leadership
- Lighthearted nature
- Change
- Multitasking
- Confidence
- Negotiating
- Opportunistic
- Adapting
- Persuasion
- Energy and endurance
- Resilience
- Engaging
- Risk-taking
- Self-expression
- Generating ideas
- Spontaneity
- Influencing and promoting
- Troubleshooting
- Decisiveness
- Visionary

JOYS

Promoters gain satisfaction, fulfillment, and joy from the following:

- Adventures and activities
- Being generous
- Performing
- Being recognized for individual success
- Competing and being the best
- Excitement and fun
- Moving their body or dancing
- Coping with problems and crisis
- Putting plans into action
- Taking risks
- Troubleshooting
- Choice and variety
- Being in charge or leading
- Freedom
- Attention
- Personal indulgences
- Using tool

VALUES

Values are an inner guide that directs a Promoter's actions and gives their life purpose and meaning.

- Instinct for opportunity
- Adventure, change, and variety
- Productivity – getting things done immediately
- Hands-on experiences
- Risk-taking and being bold
- Competition and winning
- Individual achievement and rewards
- Physical activities
- Humor, excitement, and fun
- Aesthetics
- Spontaneity
- Creativity
- Forthrightness
- Flexibility
- Challenge
- Action

CORE VALUE: Freedom

NEEDS

Meeting a Promoter's needs is a sure way to gain their cooperation. Their comfort, health, happiness, and success, depends on satisfying these needs through continued opportunities and experiences. When their needs are not satisfied, frustration and stress increase, which often leads to conflict; or worse, emotional or physical health problems.

- Independence and freedom to do as they like
- Direct communication – no game playing
- To talk and express themselves; sharing stories, jokes, and experiences
- To be noticed and shown attention
- To seize opportunities; act on a moment's notice; be productive and make things happen
- Humor and playfulness
- Immediate feedback; straightforward answers

- Informal environment
- Physical movement and mobility
- To be skillful; have mastery of tools and hands-on activities
- To receive recognition for performance, skills, and ideas
- Involvement and social contact
- To engage in entertainment and fun
- To attain tangible rewards
- To network and be resourceful; meet needs
- To be spontaneous; be able to switch gears with little thought
- To negotiate; gain cooperation from others
- Challenge, competition, risk, boldness
- An adrenalin rush
- Variety and options to choose from
- Flexibility and change

STRESSORS

A Promoter's capacity to succeed in life is significantly diminished when they experience the following:

- Lack of freedom or choices
- Inflexibility; especially with time
- Unchallenging activities
- Lack of humor and play
- Repetition and unnecessary routine
- Inactivity and waiting
- Rules and regulations that bog them down
- Paperwork; being stuck at a desk
- Inability to negotiate or change outcome
- Feeling trapped or bored
- Lack of money and resources
- Not being allowed to talk or participate
- Criticism, negativity, nagging
- Indecisiveness
- Reading instructional manuals

- Lack of physical movement
- Being told what to do or how to do it
- Slow people
- Rigidity

REACTION TO STRESS

When Promoters are overwhelmed from stress their personalities no longer sparkle, and their positive attributes quickly fade. In this state, they often break the rules, act rude, and display anger, lying or cheating behavior. To return to their fun-loving state and get back on track, they need someone to encourage them to take action, move forward, and get out of their current environment to experience something new. They are quick to recover but sometimes need a little push to move forward.

When experiencing low self-esteem or stress, they may behave in the following ways:

- Overcommit and under deliver
- Display lying and cheating behavior
- Unrestrained and noisy behavior
- Act, or speak before considering consequences
- Blame, point fingers to faults of others
- Sarcastic, hurtful, mocking of others
- Stubborn, demanding of their way
- Look for an escape and will quit, drop out or detach, not caring if they burn a bridge
- Defiant or rude outbursts
- Purposely break rules
- Demonstrate anger and aggressive behavior
- Use manipulation to get what they want
- Avoids taking action, due to boredom
- Use avoidance behavior
- Seek immediate gratification or quick fix of outside stimulants

- Reject advice
- Seek escape from reality by daydreaming
- Impulsive – moves from one thing to another without completing anything

TURN TO PROMOTERS FOR:

Ideas and Inspiration – Promoters are playful and like to brainstorm ideas. Their creative brains act as idea machines, spewing new ideas out at a rapid rate. They get excited when asked to contribute their thoughts and can quickly generate fun suggestions for family gatherings, conferences or any event. When they are excited, their enthusiasm and optimism inspire everyone around them.

Leadership – Promoters are confident leaders. Put them into any situation, with little experience, and they'll make it work. Their innovative brains figure things out as they go, producing top results every time. They think out of the box and are not afraid to take a risk and try new things.

Getting Things Done Immediately – Promoters are all about seizing the opportunity and taking immediate action. They do well with sudden change and can switch directions at the turn of a dime. They are optimistic, innovative and gifted at finding shortcuts. When you want things done quickly, ask a Promoter.

Resourcefulness – They are social, love small talk and networking. Promoters have a massive database of connections and people to draw from. If they don't have an immediate answer, they know someone who knows someone else who has the resource you need. They are very outgoing and interactive, building relationships wherever they go.

Problem-solving - As natural-born trouble-shooters, they remain calm during a crisis. When there is a problem, they immediately jump into solution mode. They are independent and make quick decisions. They have a knack for harnessing talents in others, delegating tasks as necessary to keep everything under control. No one can generate ideas and solutions faster than a Promoter.

Skillful Use of Tools – They are hands-on people who have the ability to accurately build and create things that provide a more pleasant life for others. They may be a creative workshop leader, an award-winning hair stylist, a recognized artist, the builder of notable buildings or even cities. They perform their cutting-edge ideas with ease and precision.

Motivation – Their excitement is contagious, and they use their charm to motivate people to participate with them. They have a knack for enrolling everyone in their vision, inspiring them to take action when required. They are confident, and people want to do what they do.

Adventure and Entertainment – Their energy and optimism come through in their adventures and when they have the opportunity to entertain someone. Their sharing is usually in story form, filled with larger-than-life examples, and expressions that keep their audience entertained. Life is an adventure for a Promoter and they want to share it with you. If there is an event, enroll their participation and they will ensure it is a memorable one.

Fun and Laughter – Promoters are light-hearted, quick-witted and laugh more than any of the other personality styles. Their child-like character can even find the humor in the mundane and unpleasant. Because humor is part of their DNA, they cheer others up naturally. They love creating fun and laughter everywhere they go.

Negotiation – Gaining the cooperation of others and turning a "no" into a "yes" comes naturally for the Promoter personality style. Their creative minds will present a continuous stream of options necessary to reach their goal - rarely do they ever need to compromise.

Forthright Response – Promoters are straightforward and tell it like it is. They are not afraid to have an opinion, even when it is not a popular one; they give you their uncensored response with little concern about being politically correct.

CHALLENGE – Motivated by their natural competitive nature and sense of fun they play full-out in any competition and play to win. A challenge keeps things interesting and gives them a chance to pull out all the stops with their innovative ideas. Their optimism helps keep things enjoyable.

TASKS REQUIRING Risk – Promoters are courageous and have no fear of taking risks. They make risky investments and like daring adventures like bungee jumping, fire walking, or skydiving. They are bold and fearless and often do things for the sheer enjoyment they get from the accompanying adrenaline rush. They feel alive when they test the limits.

VARIETY – Promoters get bored quickly and therefore create new and innovative ways of doing things to feed their voracious appetite for variety. Variety is the spice of life they say. They love to travel, experience new foods, adventures, fashion, etc., and will share their experiences, giving others who aren't quite as experimental some new options to try.

RECREATION – Promoters like to be active, and they need to be in motion. They have a zest for life and are the first to try new things. They need to use up their physical energy and are therefore involved in several activities where they can push and exert themselves. Going to the gym, mountain bike riding or extreme sports, all appeal to a Promoter.

PROMOTION AND SALES – They can promote and sell almost anything to anyone. When they believe in something, look out! Their enthusiasm and the way they present the possibilities persuade even the most difficult to convince. Top sales people in most companies are likely Promoters.

SPONTANEITY – Because they have no issues with change, they will drop what they are doing to participate without hesitation. They enjoy the stimulation, freedom, and the excitement of something new. If plans change, or they get a spur-of-the-moment invitation, they will optimistically go with the flow.

GENEROSITY – Promoters are generous with their finances, time, energy, and ideas. They like to give extravagant gifts. Their creative minds like to give the unexpected and wrap it with artistic flair. They go beyond expectations in their job or extra-curricular activities.

CHAPTER 9

MEET THE PLANNER PERSONALITY STYLE

Planners are among the most disciplined of all four personality types. They are self-motivated and results-oriented. If they have a goal in mind, nothing will stand in their way. They are the ones who sign up for a gym pass and attend on a regular basis. They are the people who set a goal to lose ten pounds and accomplish it. They are the worker bees that bring projects to realization. They are incredibly productive and love the feeling they get from accomplishing things. Getting results energizes them to take on more duties and responsibilities.

Planners like familiar routine and appreciate knowing what to expect. The more often they do something in a particular way; the more likely they are to adopt the pattern. Often, they will eat a certain type of meal every day for breakfast or lunch, without entertaining a change. If something works, they stick with it. They have the most difficult time of all four personality styles with change. They prefer things that work stay the same. They rely heavily on past precedent, both behaviorally and when relating to ideas. Once they have established a routine, they don't want it changed or discontinued.

Typically, Planners are relatively serious and offer little in the arena of spontaneity or humor. That doesn't mean they can't have fun, but for the most part, the fun has to be scheduled. They are reserved and take longer to warm up to people and can sometimes be viewed as cold, bossy, stubborn, inflexible, or nitpicky, but are more easygoing than people credit them for being. They may also appear unfriendly and uninterested, and that is because they always have a planned agenda to tend to, they want people to "cut to the chase" as time is valuable to them. Once their tasks are handled, they will make time for you.

Planners are loyal to their friends and partners and gravitate towards people who embrace a similar lifestyle and world view. Despite their outer confidence and imposing presence, they are often inwardly insecure and not sure of themselves. They are the most judgmental of all four personality styles, which is mainly due to their lack of internal control. A Planner experiences anxiety when they sense that they are not in control, hence their propensity for restlessness and hypervigilance.

Being on time is critical for the Planner personality style. As a matter of fact, they are the ones that show up ten minutes early for an appointment. They do not like it when others are late and expect their friends and co-workers to show up at the agreed-upon time. They especially get irritated at the Promoter personality types who are frequently late. Planners expect scheduled meetings to start as scheduled as they dislike wasting time, no matter what the excuse is.

The Planner personality style is a stickler for service. They give exceptional service and expect the same in return. They will get annoyed with retail clerks who ignore them and will not hesitate to file a complaint to the person in charge whenever their experience is less than excellent. Their purpose for doing so is to help others improve the service they provide.

They are driven and have a long list of things to accomplish, often appearing rushed or unapproachable due to their focus. When they are focused, they only want to give time to the things on their list. When they are busy, they may not listen well if you interrupt them, especially to small talk. They are very direct in their communication and want to get straight to the point.

Relaxing is difficult for a Planner because there is always work to do. They schedule relaxation and play time with activities that are structured, organized and well-planned. To Planners, there is a right and wrong way to do everything, including how to play games. They are rule-bound and will be quick to point out violations or errors when participating in any games and expect everyone to adhere to the rules if they are to play.

Planners strive to be their word and practice what they preach. They are steadfast in all their commitments. They value security and save money for their children's education and their future needs. They know what their bank account balance is at any given time and will always stick to their budget. They only make a purchase when it's necessary and planned, and will look for the best deal, buying items on sale whenever possible.

Because Planners are self-sufficient and responsible, they frown at those who take advantage of other people's generosity, labeling them as freeloaders or takers. They want to be the providers, not the receivers, of service or charity. Should they ever accept a helping hand; they will be quick to devise a plan to repay their provider. Staying debt-free is a high priority.

Structure and safety are huge values for Planners. They take these seriously and will labor tirelessly to ensure they are intact both at home and work. They will set plans in place should there be an earthquake, flood, or emergency; ensuring that everyone knows their precise role and what to do if any of these events occur. Safety also includes being financially prepared for emergencies and retirement.

Social status is often a high priority for Planners. Although tight-fisted with their money, they will spend money on a nice car and home. They like quality and will purchase items that have longevity; they will save, until they can afford to buy whatever they want. As far as their dress goes, they are conservative and prefer to invest in classic clothing that they can wear for years to come.

They like everything to be consistent and predictable in their lives and feel best in an orderly and stable environment. Their homes are clean, neat and tidy. These people have a place for everything, and everything is in its place. They are master organizers who gain energy every time they check off an item on their 'to-do' list. Getting things done takes priority over play.

Planners are sticklers for manners! They know proper etiquette and have high expectations in this area. They are very appropriate for everything they do and like to keep things professional, especially in any dealings they have with people outside their home environment. They are very determined and reliable, but may appear domineering, and demanding when their focus is interrupted.

A Planner will bring order to chaos, staying calm and unemotional while focusing on a practical solution. They are detailed, dutiful, and realistic. They will consider the facts before they reach a conclusion and can be counted on to get the job done right.

Another attribute the Planner personality style possesses is accountability. They are ethical, honest, and conscientious. They do what they say they will do and can always be depended on for accuracy and following through to make responsible decisions.

They plan ahead for trips, packing a few weeks in advance. If they are going away, they will book the hotel months ahead of time to get the best deal. They start making a list of what needs to be done immediately after a decision to do something is made and continually review and add new items to it, making sure nothing is left out.

Planners gravitate towards careers that are structured and predictable, positions where they act as guardians, such as management positions, legal positions (police), financial planners, teachers, or political positions. Many work in business, banking, service occupations, military or civil service. Because social standing is important to them, they prefer to associate with prominent people and established, recognized institutions.

Planners defend as well as preserve traditions and conventions, especially familiar ones. Commonly they will carry on traditions that they grew up with, including sticking with their childhood religion and they will continue to pass these beliefs and customs on to their family. They value family time and run an organized and planned lifestyle, ensuring they allocate time for family activities and friendships.

Planners respect their elders and honor the chain of command in the family and other areas of life. They teach their children responsibility from a young age, and chores are assigned early on. No child of theirs will ever be lazy, nor will they ever depend on others to pay their way. They teach their children that they must do their part as one's status must be earned.

Planners are self-disciplined and responsible and can be counted on to do their duty. They ensure that what others create is implemented, with everything running smoothly. They organize everything, provide directives, ensure rules are adhered to, and help people to be accountable, doing what they are supposed to do. They are efficient and meticulous, providing detailed plans that help bring completion to projects. They are dependable; the worker bees that stay committed and focused on finishing the job.

A PLANNER'S GIFTS

All of us are here to use our gifts to make a contribution to the world. A dominant Planner's gifts are a natural part of their DNA, making them effortless to use. Most of their gifts involve preserving, enforcing, or doing something, which is their primary purpose in life.

They are loyal and represent duty, responsibility, and guidance. When Planners are allowed to express their unique gifts, it contributes to their overall success and happiness.

- Following directions
- Providing safety and security
- Being practical
- Etiquette
- Bringing order to chaos
- Structure and routine
- Dutiful and goal-oriented
- Dependability
- Loyal
- Detail-oriented nature
- Efficient and precise
- Enforcing rules, regulations, policies and procedures
- Accountability
- Family-oriented
- Commitment
- Law abiding
- Discipline
- Managing
- Organization – creating systems and order
- Saving time, money, or resources
- Preserving customs and traditions
- Scheduling
- Administration
- Providing sound judgment

- Planning
- Self-motivation
- Being punctual
- Responsible and reliable
- Realistic mindset

- Ethical
- Stability
- Completion
- Honesty
- Trustworthiness

JOYS

Planners gain satisfaction, fulfillment, and joy from the following:

- Security
- Being prepared
- Completion of tasks
- A sense of belonging
- Establishing routines
- Timelines
- Fairness
- Time for family

- Home
- Tradition and heritage
- Providing stability
- Reaching closure
- A sense of order
- Tangible rewards
- Doing the "right thing"
- Job satisfaction

VALUES

Values are an inner guide that directs a Planner's actions and gives their life purpose and meaning.

- Status
- Commitment
- Practical decisions and common sense
- Etiquette, formality, and professionalism
- Accomplishment
- Standards
- Duty and responsibility

- Being on time
- Religious heritage
- Morality
- Family traditions
- Loyalty
- Honesty and integrity
- Time and resources
- Order and organization
- Security, safety, and stability

- Routines
- Rules, policies, and procedure

CORE VALUE: Responsibility

NEEDS

Meeting a Planner's needs is a sure way to gain their cooperation. Their comfort, health, happiness, and success, depends on satisfying these needs through continued opportunities and experiences. When their needs are not satisfied, frustration and stress increase, which often leads to conflict; or worse, emotional or physical health problems.

- To plan before engaging in activities
- Respect, appreciation, and acknowledgment
- To adhere to rules, regulations, policies, procedures, and laws
- A structured formal environment
- To show loyalty and commitment to family, friends, and employer
- Orderliness, organization, and cleanliness
- Safety, stability, and security
- To get results – get things done; check items off on their "to-do-list"
- To preserve tradition, heritage, and customs
- Proper etiquette - formal and professional
- To follow routine
- To be economic; save time, money, and resources
- To do the right thing
- Consistency – rely on the tried and true
- Reliability and accuracy
- Honest communication
- To be punctual
- Clearly defined boundaries, roles, requirements, expectations, and timelines
- To attain closure and completion
- To be realistic and practical

STRESSORS

A Planner's capacity to succeed in life is significantly diminished when they experience the following:

- Carrying most of the responsibilities
- Being surprised
- Taking risks
- Time pressure – being rushed
- Lack of control
- Incomplete tasks or conversations
- No savings account
- Unnecessary or unplanned change
- Too many things going on at the same time
- People who are late
- Indecisiveness
- Disorganization and chaos
- Interruptions
- Waste of time, money or resources
- Not knowing what the plan is
- Having to be spontaneous
- Irresponsibility
- Procrastination
- Unfulfilled expectations or dishonesty
- People who don't follow through

REACTION TO STRESS

When Planners are overwhelmed or feel pressure, their personalities can be a challenge to face. Their good traits quickly disappear as they try to regain their footing. In this state they often complain and behave with self-pity, blaming others for their problems. They exhibit anxiety and worry, and their judgment of self and others can become quite malicious. They become bossy in an attempt to gain back control of their environment. To help a Planner recover this loss of power, encourage them to take the time to reach clarity about what needs to happen. Pointing out their value and reminding them that they are important will help them move forward.

When experiencing low self-esteem or stress, they may behave in the following ways:

- Being domineering and bossy, "I know better than you" attitude
- Displaying a pessimistic outlook
- Judgmental of self and others
- Self-righteous, right about everything
- Impatient
- Arrogant - insensitivity to feelings
- Short tempered
- Stubborn, rigid and inflexible
- Resistant to change
- Exhibits anxiety and worry
- Fatigued and depressed
- Blame others for the stress they feel
- Gossip about others when they are angry at them
- Tattletales, pointing out others' wrongs
- Verbally aggressive, short and blunt in their communication
- Black and white thinking
- Threatening and demanding
- Complain and feel sorry for themselves

TURN TO PLANNERS FOR:

Administration – They are professional in every sense and know proper etiquette in business and at home, having high standards in these regions. They steer others towards the accomplishment of goals and directives by planning, organizing and supervising others.

Service – Planners are great in service-type organizations to identify tasks that are incomplete, using available resources to get the job done. The services they provide are more task-focused than people-focused.

Tradition, Heritage, and History – They like things to remain the same and therefore hold their heritage in high regard. At home, they continue traditions from their childhood and do their utmost to preserve their family history. They are devoted and loyal to family, friends and their place of work. They also work at maintaining the culture and traditions of the country they live in, the place they work, and any service groups where they have a membership.

Doing Things Right – Be it manners or the correct way to do something, a Planner is usually well-informed. They believe there is a right and wrong way for most everything. They are self-disciplined, and independent, taking pride in knowing what is appropriate and traditional while doing things the right way.

Planning Events or Projects – They are gifted at knowing what needs doing and will create a step-by-step plan to ensure the event or project is completed correctly and on time. When planning an event, working with a Supporter can be a great combination, as long as they stay away from the creative planning and focus on the logistics and budgetary needs. They are great at making practical decisions and setting realistic timelines for completion.

Teaching – Planners like to instruct others in a systematic way and will follow the rules of the curriculum to ensure their pupils get the full training they deserve. They enjoy it when others advance in their knowledge on the subjects they teach.

Responsibility and Duty – They are independent, self-disciplined, dependable and reliable. Planners get energized by results; they like to be busy and thrive on having a full plate of "to-do's." They work hard and gain great pleasure from setting goals and executing them with excellence. They always do what they say they will do and can be counted on to deliver results in a timely fashion.

Management – Planners can be put in charge of a vision or project and will make a detailed plan to include all the necessary steps required to bring the project to fruition. They manage all aspects of a project by providing direction to others, ensuring the plan is accomplished with accuracy.

ORGANIZATION – Planners value order and are masters at establishing systems that contribute to things working better; be it a system for your goals, files, time, or things. You can put a Planner in utter chaos and they will straighten it out, being happy doing it. They keep things neat and tidy.

SAVING TIME AND MONEY – Planners are always punctual. Because time is valuable to them, they are masters at using it wisely. When there is work to do they won't be sitting around chatting about life; instead, they will have their nose buried in the task at hand. Planners are security conscious and when it comes to money and budgets, they like to save; knowing how to cut corners and delighting in coming in under budget with money to spare. To save time or money in any situation, Planners can help. They are frugal and know where to find a bargain.

DETAILS – They are gifted at taking a complicated project or task and breaking it down into a detailed step-by-step process. Their brains work in such a way that they can speculate all the necessary elements required to complete the tasks, without missing any steps. They cross the "T's" and dot the "I's" leaving no detail unattended.

HONESTY – Planners are ethical, trustworthy and confidential. They like truth and rarely tell a lie. They dislike gossip and negative talk about others and are loyal to those they respect. You can ask them a question and you'll get a straight, honest answer. At work, they are trusted with financial information and budgets.

Policy, Procedures, and Rules – They like to know what the policies, procedures, and rules are so they can be compliant with them. They are law abiding in all areas. They are often instrumental in the design and implementation of policies, procedures, and rules, especially if they are non-existent.

Accuracy – Planners are perfectionists and like everything completed correctly. Because they are sticklers for detail, they will ensure they check and double-check their work to ensure its accuracy. They don't like guessing and like to base everything on fact. They make great proofreaders and can keep track of cash or a budget with precision. Rarely will they make an error.

Scheduling – Planners live their lives on a timetable. They plan everything, and as a result, they always have a "to-do" list on the go. They accomplish a lot because of their organized scheduling of tasks and events. If they have something scheduled, you can count on them to show up or get the job done. They are clock watchers, because to them every minute counts.

Fairness – As long as everyone follows the rules, they are usually very reasonable. They have a sense of justice and will pay careful attention to what is just and impartial. In situations that need discipline, they will consider all the facts before imparting what the correct action should be to remedy the problem.

Creating Routine and Structure – Planners thrive on the predictable and hence, love structure and routine. At home, they usually get up at the same time every day and follow the same routine they've had for years. At work, they will be on time and will have regular, systematic methods for completing their daily duties. When a new routine needs to be created and implemented, a Planner will handle it like a pro.

Direct to the Point Communication – Planners don't want to spend a lot of time talking about the task or project because they want to get to doing it instead. Because they value time more than any of the four personality styles, they prefer getting to the point in a conversation. They are very direct when they speak and have little need for connecting on a personal level when there is a job to be done.

Chapter 10

Meet the Thinker Personality Style

Thinkers value intelligence and are usually well educated. They may not always have college or university degrees, but their ferocious appetites for learning ensure they stay well informed on topics of interest. They often received good grades in school, score high on IQ tests and may hold leadership roles as well.

Thinkers are known for their extensive vocabularies and impeccable grammar. They enjoy the written word and often prefer to express themselves fully and precisely through writing, because it gives them an outlet to sort through their thoughts and time to convey them completely.

Play rarely occurs to a Thinker. They have a tendency to take life seriously, using their inner logic to navigate and discern as they go. For them, work becomes play, especially acquiring knowledge that will carry their goals forward. That's not to say they don't know how to have fun! Thinkers love new experiences and will seek them out. In many cases, they enjoy extreme sports; like skiing black diamond runs, hiking Everest, or backpacking in a third world country.

When Thinkers go on vacation, they seek out different experiences from the norm; exploring new cultures, restaurants, ethnic foods or new sites while thoroughly enjoying the discoveries they make along the way. They enjoy travel and will know months ahead of time where they want to go, as their research is a big part of their fun and relaxation.

Thinkers are continuous learners. It is uncommon to find a Thinker without a library membership, a Kindle or a similar item giving quick access to the books they love. They are avid readers from a young age and always have several books on the go at once. Although they can access books electronically, they greatly prefer traditional books, rarely parting with the hundreds they acquire. Thinkers are the people who keep bookstores in business and will gladly spend a whole day combing their shelves.

Not only do they love books, but they also love technology. They will have the latest technological devices, know all their functions and can give you the reasons that their device is the best. They do their homework before making a purchase and are therefore an excellent resource for those who are not as technologically savvy.

Because their brains are wired to connect the dots, they are most often the very people who create modern technology, programs, apps, and games. When learning a new program or app, logically they will want to know each step of its function and why it functions the way it does – it's how they learn.

Many Thinkers are musically inclined, which is a wonderful outlet for energy and emotion. Most Thinkers enjoy music and have an extensive and varied collection of old and new tunes. They value a premium stereo which allows them to hear the lyrics and musical tones clearly. Music can become a comfortable way to be social for them, and many play in a symphony or band.

A high percentage of Thinkers are introverted, often feeling self-conscious and awkward in a social setting. Many display anxious or nervous behaviors, showing how tense they feel. Having direct eye contact makes them feel uneasy; instead, they will look in another direction, often making the person they are communicating with feel uncomfortable as well. At large gatherings, they may stand back and observe, and will usually engage in conversation with a person possessing a similar nature to their own. They have a knack for finding one another in a crowd and rarely partake in group discussions, unless it is about a topic they are well-versed in.

Thinkers avoid small talk at all cost. When forced to endure it, they will quickly zone out or redirect the conversation. Many find discussing personal issues and the details of people's lives rather annoying and uncomfortable;

instead, they are more interested in discussing ideas and discoveries. They prefer to converse about things based on facts, ideas, histories or past illustrations.

They like to do lots of things; but rarely will they participate in anything until they feel competent. They prefer to read or research rather than watching sports. Their greatest vulnerability is to look stupid or made a fool of, and they will do anything to avoid either one.

Thinkers are prone to be somewhat distant. They feel emotions deeply; however, few provide many clues regarding their reaction to situations. They are very feeling-based like Supporters. A Supporter likes to share personal feelings in connecting with others, and Thinkers make decisions based on their sense of security. When they feel any insecurity, Thinkers rely on data gathering to feel confident they have enough evidence for evaluating the situation. Though they hide their emotions for safety and protection, Thinkers are not void of deep feelings.

Most are loners that like to have peace and quiet and do not do well in a crowded or noisy area. They need to have space where they can have much-needed time alone to process and contemplate. As a matter of fact, if they have spent time in a crowd, they will need extra quiet, alone time to regenerate and rejuvenate. Out of all four personality styles, the Thinkers enjoy their own company the most.

Thinkers are very curious and spend much of their time working to discern unifying themes and metaphysical truths that explain the underlying nature of things and how they work. They research and devour stacks of books on a topic and accurately assess all the constituent parts. It is important for them to understand the whole picture. Topics that interest them may be technology, philosophy, math, mechanics, engineering, psychology, religion or any science-based subject. Many people feel challenged and intellectually inadequate in a Thinker's presence.

They are motivated to understand the world around them and desire to explain, forecast and apply control over reality. Thinkers are natural scientists, people who explore and define the limitations of natural law. They want to know how things work in detail, the reason behind everything, and will work endlessly to reach solid conclusions.

Thinkers like solving problems by asking questions, by researching and coming up with new ideas and by using models. They need clear objectives and enough time to gather data and information, as well as time to analyze it before making a decision. Because their thinking is objective, they won't be satisfied with simple explanations but need to understand the principle or theory behind concepts. They need autonomy and like to work on projects independently.

Thinkers do not like having to make quick, uninformed decisions or being given unclear goals. They are quick to point out repetition or redundancy, having little patience for either.

Thinkers are serious and purposeful, the profound and brilliant minds of the world. They relate well to others through information and can have a reputation of boring people with too many details. Their challenge is to cultivate their social skills, learn how to show more emotion when they communicate and to acquire the skills of reading body language to gauge interest in what they are sharing.

They also have a quirky sense of humor and often use sarcastic remarks directed at a particular person in their banter. Their dry wit and sarcasm are frequently misunderstood by recipients, often causing them to react and bite back. Thinkers only strike when attacked or angry, and when they do they use devastating blows that are intended to shut the other party up. It's their defense – but thankfully it is rarely used, only when they are out of self-esteem.

It is not uncommon for a Thinker to take the opposite viewpoint during a conversation to keep things interesting. They enjoy a healthy debate and delight in arguing their point of view. Some see this as antagonistic, but they see it as entertainment.

Thinkers serve others with their vast knowledge, vision, and innovation to improve performance and make significant changes in the world. They seek to improve systems in areas such as education, technology, politics, government or moving a company or project forward. They have minds that never quit and dream up new things and ideas that others have not thought of yet. Their ability to conceptualize before creating something gives them a clear edge. Though motivated by the pure acquisition of knowledge; control of their education is equally important to them, because they deem knowledge as power.

Thinkers derive much of their self-esteem from work. They are extremely focused and take their jobs very seriously. As mentioned earlier, most consider their work as play. Suitable careers for the Thinker personality are those that require intellect, vision, and independent thinking. Being gifted at conceptualizing, theorizing, and coordinating complex issues, they gravitate towards areas that need logical investigation. Many consider careers in law, accounting, medicine, science, technology, engineering, assisting a physician or maybe in mechanics. Most college or university professors are of this quadrant of people because once they learn something, they feel compelled to share their knowledge. Whatever career choice they make, they strive to be the best at it, often rising to the top in their profession and/or organization.

Thinkers are resourceful and always manage to get into careers that pay well. They plan ahead for their financial future and will only make a purchase when it's necessary. They will always research before making a purchase to ensure they get the best quality and value.

Competence and clarity of thought are a Thinker's chief assets. They comprise a small percentage of the population of bright people who are independent, creative, solution-oriented, cool-headed, and most often non-conforming. They are the Einsteins of the world. Thinkers are the ones who chart new territory and make discoveries that often have global impact.

A THINKER'S GIFTS

All of us are here to use our gifts to make a contribution to the world. A dominant Thinker's gifts are a natural part of their DNA, making them effortless to use. Most of their gifts involve using their knowledge and competence to analyze, solve problems or invent something better, which is their primary purpose in life.

They are conceptual and represent ingenuity, persistence, and change. When Thinkers are allowed to express their unique gifts, it contributes to their overall success and happiness.

- Abstract thinking
- Competence
- Debating and questioning
- Philosophical ideas
- Visionary
- Persistent and determined
- Systematic insights
- Innovation
- Developing systems and models
- Evaluating and investigating
- Precise spelling and grammar
- Improving upon status quo
- Technical know-how
- Unemotional advice
- Intellectual triumphs
- Knowledge
- Logic
- Strategic processing
- Analyzing
- Making decisions based on facts
- Objectivity
- Insightfulness
- Perfectionism
- Conceptualizing
- Precise, concise, accurate work
- Generating ideas
- Independent processing
- Problem solving, fixing things
- Exploring
- Researching
- Self-control - cool, calm, collected
- Inventing
- Theoretical ideas
- Diagnosing
- Witty, dry humor

JOYS

Thinkers gain satisfaction, fulfillment, and joy from the following:

- Being acknowledged by professional colleagues
- Exploring new ideas
- Being recognized for original systems and new ideas
- High achievement and superior accomplishments
- Meeting challenges
- Understanding and explaining complexities
- Solving problems
- Discovering new possibilities
- Demonstrating technical expertise
- Doing what can't be done
- Creative freedom

- Humor and irony
- Time to think and analyze
- Research and reading to gain knowledge

VALUES

Values are an inner guide that directs a Thinker's actions and gives their life purpose and meaning.

- Accuracy
- Knowledge, wisdom, and expertise
- Intellectual achievement
- Logic
- Creativity
- Ingenuity
- Independence
- Analysis
- Ideas
- Precision
- Technology
- Self-control
- Self-sufficiency
- Innovation
- Truth and facts, data, information, and statistics
- Systematic approach
- Strategy
- Improvement

Core Value: Competence

NEEDS

Meeting a Thinker's needs is a sure way to gain their cooperation. Their comfort, health, happiness, and success, depends on satisfying these needs through continued opportunities and experiences. When their needs are not satisfied, frustration and stress increase, which often leads to conflict; or worse, emotional or physical health problems.

- Privacy – peace and quiet
- To find solutions and make improvements
- Challenge – do what others say can't be done
- Autonomy - time to think, read, analyze

- Intellectual stimulation
- Facts, truth, and accuracy
- Information, data, and statistics
- To explore new ideas
- Research; being well-informed
- Flexibility
- Correct speech and grammar
- To be curious, inquiring, questioning, and skeptical
- To be objective
- To gain knowledge and wisdom; continually improving and learning
- Innovation – improving the status quo and creating change
- To make comparisons; look at pros and cons
- Competence, logic and sound reasoning
- Systems and technology that work well
- To be emotionally composed – not swayed by emotions or feelings
- To develop, diagnose, design, and invent

STRESSORS

A Thinker's capacity to succeed in life is significantly diminished when they experience the following:

- Senseless or unreasonable rules
- Emotional displays without logic
- Chaos and confusion
- Rigidity
- Lack of independence or freedom
- Appearing stupid
- Being unprepared or having to make quick decisions
- Incompetence in self or others
- Routine, redundancy and repetition
- Unclear goals and objectives
- Unfairness
- Equipment or technology failure

- Bad grammar
- Inability to display or use knowledge
- Loud noises and distractions
- Social functions and small talk
- Not knowing, understanding or having answers
- Mistakes
- Lack of options or time to properly analyze, study or gather data
- Judgments made based on beliefs or feelings, rather than verifiable evidence of facts
- Individuals who don't value wisdom, knowledge, and learning

REACTION TO STRESS

When Thinkers are stressed out or overwhelmed their personalities grow dim, and their positive characteristics do an about face. In this state, they often behave indecisively and will withdraw and stop communicating. They usually refuse to comply and get highly critical towards self and others. Many obsess and worry. To rebuild their self-esteem, they need time alone and someone to encourage them by pointing out their value, intelligence, and contribution.

When experiencing low self-esteem or stress, they may behave in the following ways:

- Insensitivity to feelings of others
- Contrary questioning
- Playing victim
- Becoming impatient
- Disapproval towards self and others
- Using words as a weapon to cut others down
- Withdrawing and distancing themselves
- Stubbornly refusing to comply or cooperate
- Analysis paralysis
- Feeling like no one gets them or understands them
- Breaking rules
- Having angry outbursts

- Blaming others, circumstances or technology
- Arrogant and argumentative attitude
- Depressed state

TURN TO THINKERS FOR:

ANALYTICAL Skill – Thinkers are known to make sensible decisions by gathering required data and information. While pouring over information, they have the ability to visualize, articulate, conceptualize or solve the most complex of problems.

PERFECTION – They are very efficient and always look for ways to improve something. They are only happy when they have perfected their work.

FIXING THINGS – Thinkers are gifted at diagnosing problems and figuring out how to repair or fix things.

LOGICAL REASONING – Thinkers form sound judgments and conclusions by assessing a situation using logic, knowledge and proven methods of reasoning.

DEVELOPING SYSTEMS – Using a logical process, they plan, design, test and deploy new systems. Most software, engineering, or information systems were created by Thinkers. They are very methodical and will develop one step at a time.

PERSISTENCE – A Thinker does not give up easily. They will persevere, evaluating every aspect of how something works to come up with a viable result. Like Thomas Edison, if they don't get it right the first time, they persist until they get it right; always thinking, studying and learning better ways of doing things.

INVENTING – Thomas Edison stands as the greatest inventor of all time, and he was a Thinker. He would define a need and work on finding the solution. Thinkers follow the same pattern, using their analytical skills to identify a need, or problem, and work until a viable, practical answer is found and tested for efficiency. The greatest technological advances we enjoy today were likely the invention of a Thinker.

RESEARCHING – A Thinker can spend countless hours researching topics of interest with no concept of the time that has passed. They are thorough re-searchers who know where to find useful information. They always have a plethora of interesting topics they want to research and could easily spend an entire day doing so.

TECHNICAL KNOW HOW – Because their brains work in an analytical, systematic way, they can conceptualize how technical things work by connecting the dots. If you have a technical problem, they most often can fix it.

COMPETENCE – Because Thinkers have no margin for error, they educate themselves by gathering and studying information and data until they are confident that they come across as an expert, or at least as competent. They ensure that the fields they work in, or the discussions they have regarding an issue originate from a place of knowledge and education. When they do something, they do it well.

INTELLIGENCE – Thinkers are intellects. In conversations, they desire to dive into topics where they can share their knowledge and wisdom. In school, they were the nerdy academic achievers. They like information and data and never stop educating themselves on topics of interest. Their grammatical skills are far superior to the other personality styles.

VISION – Thinkers are always looking for ways to change the status quo. They are known for bringing about the world's most renowned advances, developments, and inventions by establishing new systems and protocols. They are big picture, global thinkers and therefore concern themselves with the progress that will influence society. They are the Einsteins and Edisons of the world.

CONCEPTUALIZING – Their gifted logical minds link all the necessary steps (A - Z) together. Using a systematic approach, they examine the various scenarios, being mindful of the cause and effect, until they bring a concept to fruition.

INNOVATION – Gifted at coming up with new methods and ideas. They love taking on a challenge that others can't solve and will diligently work until they find an innovative solution.

INQUISITIVE – Thinkers inquire, research and ask questions. They are naturally curious and are eager for knowledge that will help them resolve a problem or contentious matter or will assist them in charting new ground. They love to study and ask questions regarding how and why things function the way they do.

ACCURACY – Thinkers are sticklers for accuracy and have little tolerance for error. Their systematic, analytical processing helps them develop things with absolute precision. Their slow, methodical way of doing things pretty much eliminates any margin for error.

KNOWLEDGE - Their insatiable thirst for knowledge only gets heightened when they learn more about their chosen topic through research. They will gather data and information on their favored topics until they know everything about it. Once they have a thorough knowledge on a subject, they get excited and auto-matically want to share it with others.

Solving Problems - They will study the problem until they have a resolution, pouring over the research and data they have gathered to ensure their solution is achievable. The more complicated the problem, the more charged and committed they are to solving it.

PART V

Understanding Spiritual Gifts

"But each of you has your own gift from God."
1 Corinthians 7:7b

Chapter 11

✳

Spiritual Gifts

WE ARE GOD'S CREATION

With God, there is no ranking or hierarchy. We are all created equal, unique and gifted for a specific purpose.

God wants us to respect and honor each other as His creation, which can be accomplished by recognizing and understanding the differences in the traits, needs, joys, values, and stressors of the four personality styles discussed in previous chapters.

In John 15:5b, Jesus says, *"Apart from me you can do nothing,"* meaning, we need His help to accept one another without judgment, and we need His guidance to use our gifts.

God designed us to work together – to function as one body. He wants us to embrace our differences. Teaming up with those who have strengths in the areas we are weak, we can do amazing things that God has called us to do.

God's Word indicates that there are a variety of spiritual gifts. As believers, we should be aware of our gifts so we can give them to the people who need them.

WHAT IS A SPIRITUAL GIFT?

Greek: Charis or Charisma – denotes a gift is freely and graciously given, a favor bestowed, a grace. An endowment which is given by the Holy Spirit.

English Dictionary: Charism - divinely honored with, granted or bestowed with power or talent. An extraordinary power given a Christian by the Holy Spirit for the good of the church.

A spiritual gift is a supernatural ability that God gives, through the Holy Spirit, to a believer (Christian) to bring God's redeeming love into the world through service to others. Gifts are for the common good of the church, His people, to help further His work, and meet needs.

God-given gifts bring hope to our homes, our churches, and a hurting world.

DIVERSITY OF GIFTS

1 Corinthians 12:4-7 reads, *"There are <u>different kinds of gifts</u>, but the same Spirit. There are <u>different kinds of service</u>, but the same Lord. There are <u>different kinds of working</u>, but the same God works all of them in all men. Now to each one the manifestation of the Spirit is given for the common good."*

USING OUR GIFTS TO SERVE OTHERS

1 Peter 4:10-11 reads, *"<u>Each one should use whatever gift he has received to serve others</u>, faithfully administering God's grace in its various forms. If anyone speaks, he should do it as one speaking the very words of God. If anyone serves, he should do it with the strength God provides, so that in all things God may be praised through Jesus Christ. To Him be the glory and power for ever and ever."*

WHERE IN THE BIBLE ARE SPIRITUAL GIFTS DISCUSSED?

The following scriptures are the most common Biblical passages used for studying the spiritual gifts. Familiarizing yourself with these passages will help you understand the value and purpose of spiritual gifts. Additional scriptures to support each spiritual gift is found in chapter 13. P. 104

Proverbs 18:16

"A gift opens the way and ushers the giver into the presence of the great."

Romans 12:4-8

"Just as each of us has one body with many members, and these members do not all have the same function, so in Christ we who are many form one body, and each member belongs to all the others. We have different gifts, according to the grace given us. If a man's gift is prophesying, let him use it in proportion to his faith. If it is serving, let him serve; if it is teaching, let him teach; if it is encouraging; let him encourage, if it is contributing to the needs of others, let him give generously; if it is leadership, let him govern diligently; if it is showing mercy, let him do it cheerfully."

1 Corinthians 12:4-11

"There are different kinds of gifts, but the same Spirit. There are different kinds of service, but the same Lord. There are different kinds of working, but the same God works all of them in all men.

Now to each one the manifestation of the Spirit is given for the common good. To one there is given through the Spirit the message of wisdom, to another the message of knowledge by means of the same Spirit, to another faith by the same Spirit, to another gifts of healing by that one Spirit, to another miraculous powers, to another prophecy, to another distinguishing between spirits, to another speaking in different kinds of tongues, and to still another the interpretation of tongues. All these are the work of one and the same Spirit, and He gives them to each one, just as He determines."

1 Corinthians 12:27-28

"Now you are the body of Christ, and each one of you is a part of it. And in the church God has appointed first of all apostles, second prophets, third teachers, then workers of miracles, also those having gifts of healing, those able to help others, those with gifts of administration, and those speaking in different kinds of tongues."

Ephesians 4:8

"When He ascended on high, He led captives in His train and gave gifts to men."

Ephesians 4:11-16

"It was He who gave some to be apostles, some to be prophets, some to be evangelists, and some to be pastors and teachers, to prepare God's people for works of service, so that the body of Christ may be built up until we all reach unity in the faith and in the knowledge of the Son of God and become mature, attaining to the whole measure of the fullness of Christ.

Then we will no longer be infants, tossed back and forth by the waves, and blown here and there by every wind of teaching and by the cunning and craftiness of men in their deceitful scheming. Instead, speaking the truth in love, we will in all things grow up into him who is the Head, that is, Christ. From Him the whole body, joined and held together by every supporting ligament, grows and builds itself up in love, as each part does its work."

1 Peter 4:10-11

"Each one should use whatever gift he has received to serve others, faithfully administering God's grace in its various forms. If anyone speaks, he should do it as one speaking the very words of God. If anyone serves, he should do it with the strength God provides, so that in all things God may be praised through Jesus Christ. To Him be the glory and power for ever and ever. Amen."

1 Timothy 4:14

"Do not neglect your gift."

2 Timothy 1:6 NKJ

"Therefore, I remind you to stir up the gift of God which is in you…"

SPIRITUAL GIFTS ARE:

- Given without our merit, by God, because of His favor and grace (Everyone has at least one gift, with most having between two to five gifts)
- Divinely appointed – we can't pick and choose our favorites
- God's supernatural power, love, and grace flowing through believers
- Equally important – none are better or superior to other gifts
- Unique to every individual - no two people are the same
- Present at birth – not inherited from parents
- Developed and matured by God through experiences and opportunities
- Effortless and easy to use, because it's not us doing the work but the Lord
- Always a part of us - they don't retire or have an age limit
- Not earned by being good or lost if we are bad
- Fulfilling to use – accompanied by energy, excitement, creativity, joy, and peace - we feel on purpose like we've done something meaningful
- Always used for serving, helping or benefiting others; for encouragement, comfort or making a difference in the world
- Beyond our human or natural ability
- Designed to have lasting results and produce extraordinary outcomes
- Meant to give us an abundant life, not to inflict pain or rob us of life
- Not for personal adornment, status, power or popularity
- Never for evil
- Something we can't purchase – it's a gift; and if we refuse to accept the gift, it remains unopened
- To be given away; otherwise, our gifts can become a heavy burden as we recognize we are out of God's will

DIFFERENCE BETWEEN A SPIRITUAL GIFT
AND NATURAL TALENT

Our gifts grow in power and purity as we grow closer to God. Talents develop through practice and technique. Gifts are immediately and directly dependent on God's grace, while natural talents are present regardless of one's relationship with God. Gifts are purposed and intended by God to serve others; talents can be used to meet our own needs, for evil intent, or for purposes that are not about God's redeeming work. A gift is only received from God, not achieved.

WHAT IS THE PURPOSE OF SPIRITUAL GIFTS?

The purpose of spiritual gifts is not to make us spiritual, but to help us serve and minister to one another in love. When spiritual gifts are in operation, the faith of believers gets strengthened and the church functions more effectively. Any attempt we make under our own steam will prove to be fruitless, tiresome and frustrating. The Holy Spirit is our enabler and dependence on Him is essential because He works to manifest the life of Christ in us and through us, which we are incapable of doing ourselves.

Spiritual gifts provide health to the body of believers, and without them operating, the church becomes dysfunctional, which is the case of many churches today. We must never use gifts as a means of manipulating others or serving our own self-interests.

Spiritual Gifts are sacred! God has chosen to make His Spirit and His gifts dwell in our lives, so His will on earth can be accomplished. The fact that God lets us co-labor with Him by operating in our area of giftedness should excite us beyond measure. He is worthy of our praise, worship, and surrendered service!

WHO RECEIVES SPIRITUAL GIFTS?

Many believe that only the "spiritual people" receive spiritual gifts. This is, in fact, not true as they are given to believers and non-believers alike at birth but are empowered by the Holy Spirit in those who accept Jesus Christ as their Lord and Savior. Gifts are developed in a person over time, making them easy and effortless to use. Gifts are only fruitful when we seek God's leading and obey His promptings to engage them.

We were created and fashioned by the Almighty God who calls us His masterpiece and prized possession. He planted seeds of greatness inside of us while we were in our mother's womb and gave us gifts that are unique to the specific plan, purpose, and destiny He has for our life.

Take time to read, reflect, and meditate on the following scriptures:

"For we are God's masterpiece. He has created us anew in Christ Jesus, so we can do the good things he planned for us long ago." (Ephesians 2:10 NLT)

"He chose to give birth to us by giving us his true word. And we, out of all creation, became his prized possession." (James 1:18 NLT)

ARE SPIRITUAL GIFTS ONLY FOR THE CHURCH?

A church is frequently the starting place where people use their gifts. However, using a gift can happen anywhere that a born-again believer is led by the Holy Spirit to use them. The church, after all, is not a building but members of the Body of Christ.

The primary purpose of any spiritual gift is to bring Christ's love into the world.

WHAT BLOCKS THE FLOW OF SPIRITUAL GIFTS?

- Fear
- Anger
- Trying to be someone other than yourself
- Poor self-image

- Irresponsibility (not using the gifts you have)
- Pride
- Self-reliance instead of relying on God
- Sin

PART VI

Discovering Your
Spiritual Gift DNA

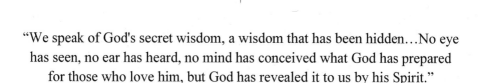

"We speak of God's secret wisdom, a wisdom that has been hidden…No eye
has seen, no ear has heard, no mind has conceived what God has prepared
for those who love him, but God has revealed it to us by his Spirit."
1 Corinthians 2:7-10

Chapter 12

✦

Spiritual Gifts Discovery Process

A starting point for discovering your spiritual gifts is prayer. Ask God which gifts he has assigned to you.

Taking a simple test called 'Discovering Your Spiritual Gift DNA' will help you discern your gifting. Below you'll find the instructions and questionnaire. The scoresheet is on the last page of this book. Making a copy of the scoresheet before you start makes the process easier.

DISCOVERING YOUR SPIRITUAL GIFT DNA

Most people have two to five gifts operating in their lives. Some are obvious, some not so obvious. Some are awake and evident, and some are asleep waiting to be awakened.

INSTRUCTIONS FOR QUESTIONNAIRE AND SCORESHEET

Respond to each question in the 'Discovering Your Spiritual Gift DNA Questionnaire' based on experiences you have actually had in your life; not on what you wish were true, or what you think should be true.

If you are struggling to respond to a question; I suggest you give it a zero. <u>Don't over analyze</u>. Give yourself 15 seconds per question at most. Score each question as honestly as you can. There is no advantage to getting high scores and no disadvantage to getting low scores. The scores only represent clues for the gift discovery process.

Once you have read a question on the questionnaire, go to the scoresheet found on the last page of the book. Look for the bold corresponding question number and circle the appropriate lighter numeral for each question as follows:

0 = Never   1 = Seldom   2 = Often   3 = Always

As you rate each question, keep in mind that skills and talents usually don't energize us when we use them; but a gift does.

When completed, add up your scores from left to right for each line and enter that number under the 'total' column on the right.

The gift names have purposely been left blank. You will receive these once you have completed the scoresheet.

Enjoy the process! You are chosen and gifted for a specific purpose!

DISCOVERING YOUR SPIRITUAL GIFT DNA QUESTIONNAIRE

Choose which number best describes you for each statement below and record your answers on the scoresheet at the end of the book.

0 = Never   1 = Seldom   2 = Often   3 = Always

---

1. I verbally encourage those who are troubled or discouraged.

2. I enjoy doing routine tasks that enable others to increase their effectiveness.

3. If I sense that someone is uncomfortable or out of place, I'll purposefully initiate a conversation with them, so they feel welcomed.

4. I help alleviate distress, improving society for those challenged with less fortunate circumstances.

5. I feel energized when I see improvement in sick or injured people under my care.

6. I often feel an urgent need to pray for people, or for particular situations.

7. I cheerfully give the best of my time, effort or finances for work that makes a difference in the world.

8. Other people have noted that I have no desire to marry or have a family.

9. I have money but choose to dress, eat and live simply.

10. I have a passion for experiencing other cultures and a desire to work with them.

11. I have confidence things will work themselves out without getting anxious about the outcome.

12. I'm very creative and have a compelling desire to make things.

13. Writing is my passion and I feel compelled to write.

14. I compose, arrange, perform, direct, produce, or teach music for the benefit of others.

15. I can immediately sense someone's underlying intentions, whether they're good or bad.

16. People come to me for advice, counsel, and solutions to problems.

17. When I make an exciting discovery through my research, I have a strong desire to share what I've learned with others.

18. I enjoy creating systems or streamlining procedures to maximize work efficiency.

19. I can visualize the final result (see the entire picture) of a project before it begins and communicate the vision in such a way that others are motivated and want to participate.

20. I'm quick to offer my physical help and don't mind doing routine or menial tasks.

21. When I passionately share my belief or cause, others are inspired to embrace and accept it.

22. I easily organize vast amounts of information, to make it easy to communicate, understand, and remember.

23. I sometimes receive revelations or visions of what is going to happen in the present or future.

24. I have enjoyed assuming the responsibility for the spiritual well-being of a particular group.

25. People are comfortable confiding their innermost thoughts and feelings with me.

26. I find it difficult to say 'No' to those who ask for help.

27. I thoroughly enjoy hosting dinners, gatherings, and social events and do so successfully.

28. I feel great compassion for the problems of others (be it humans or animals).

29. Sometimes I feel bodily heat, tingling in my hands or a strong spiritual presence when I'm treating or working with someone who wants to receive healing.

30. I pray for extended periods of time on a regular basis and see specific answers to my prayers.

31. I sense when to provide money or goods for those in less fortunate circumstances.

32. My most rewarding relationships are friendships, rather than a life partner relationship.

33. A simple lifestyle, with few possessions, brings me peace.

34. I feel comfortable relating to people from a variety of cultural backgrounds who openly accept me.

35. I've taken leaps of faith in my life because I believe everything is possible.

36. I'm artistic and creative and enjoy using my hands to build, fix or make things.

37. I like to get my ideas, thoughts, and feelings down on paper.

38. Music or singing is my preferred form of artistic expression.

39. I can sense when a negative spirit or entity is affecting a person.

40. Because my decision making has proven to be sound and correct, people seek my input.

41. I have more than one book on the go and prefer to hold on to books or reading materials.

42. I can devise and execute an efficient, effective plan for the accomplishment of required goals.

43. I work well under pressure. In the midst of stress, I make quick, effective decisions.

44. I prefer being active and doing something rather than just sitting around talking about it.

45. I can sway people by telling it like it is, causing others to see what's lacking in their lives.

46. I find joy in creating useful teaching materials.

47. I often feel as though I have a direct word from God that will comfort, encourage, guide, warn, or rebuke others.

48. I feel a desire to nurture and provide guidance and direction to others in their spiritual walk.

49. I find it easy to encourage others to recognize their highest potential.

50. I am unafraid of taking authority; however, I prefer to be in the background helping others.

51. It energizes me to have people in my home for food, lodging, and fellowship.

52. I visit prisoners, the elderly, or those who are sick to provide comfort and hope.

53. I use conventional/alternative methods or prayer to successfully treat or heal people's physical ailments.

54. Many people have told me that my prayers for them have been answered in tangible ways.

55. When I am moved by an appeal to give to a worthwhile project, I usually find the money to do so.

56. Many things that I'm called to do are only possible because I'm single.

57. I can identify and empathize with the less fortunate, and they accept me in their lives.

58. I'm drawn to other cultures and long to share experiences with them.

59. Other people have commented that I had faith to accomplish what seemed impossible to them.

60. Before I create something, I can picture how it will look once it's completed.

61. I process my experiences and express my emotions through writing.

62. I frequently listen to music paying close attention to method, expression, interpretation, etc.

63. I can accurately and quickly detect spiritual phoniness.

64. I can see several sides of an issue and sense the best way to meet the needs of a person or group.

65. I love to discover new truths for myself through research, reading, studying or observing a situation firsthand.

66. I enjoy the details of organizing ideas, people, resources or time, and do so effortlessly.

67. I bring new energy and focus to a group or project that has lost its direction.

68. I prefer not to delegate because I enjoy doing the work myself.

69.	I have witnessed others embrace the call to action and become believers and follower when sharing my persuasive message with them.

70.	When I'm teaching something to a group, I spontaneously adjust my approach to meet the learning needs of the participants.

71.	I have made accurate predictions that benefited or served others in a positive way.

72.	I have enjoyed relating to a particular group of people over a long period, sharing personally in their successes, failures, and spiritual challenges.

YOUR SPIRITUAL GIFT DNA SCORE LINEUP

Add up all the numbers horizontally on the 'Discovering Your Spiritual Gift DNA Scoresheet' and enter the sums for each line 1 to 24 under the total column. The spiritual gift names are shown below, add them to the far right-hand column (currently blank) for lines 1 to 24 on the scoresheet.

1.	Encouragement-Exhortation
2.	Helps-Assistance
3.	Hospitality
4.	Mercy-Compassion
5.	Healing
6.	Intercessory Prayer
7.	Giving
8.	Celibacy-Singleness
9.	Voluntary Poverty
10.	Missionary-Apostleship
11.	Faith-Trust
12.	Craftsmanship
13.	Writing
14.	Music
15.	Discernment

16. Wisdom
17. Knowledge
18. Administration
19. Leadership
20. Service
21. Evangelism
22. Teaching
23. Prophesy
24. Shepherding-Pastoring

Once you've added your scores, determine your spiritual gift lineup by identifying which gifts rank as your top five and enter them below.

Spiritual Gift Lineup:

Enter your highest score in #1, your second highest score in #2, etc.

1._____

2._____

3._____

4._____

5._____

Now you're ready for the gift discernment process to starts. It may take a while to correctly determine if your spiritual gift lineup is accurate, since there is more than one way to answer the questions on the 'Discovering Your Spiritual Gift DNA Questionnaire'. If you have several scores that rank in the top five due to a tie, the best thing to do is to see how you feel when you use each gift to determine which ones energize you.

✳

CHAPTER 13

24 Spiritual Gifts and Their Categories

To help clarify the accuracy of your spiritual gift lineup, read about the gifts below to see which ones resonate with you. It's a good idea to learn about all the gifts, so that you can call them forth in others. If you are weak in an area, you will want to know which gifts may complement yours. If you are planning a project, you'll know which gifts are best suited for the various roles. God designed it so that we would need each other to perform His work on earth; and when everyone collaborates, doing what they are gifted at, there is a lot of positive energy and enthusiasm.

SPIRITUAL GIFT CATEGORIES

1. Nurturing Gifts
2. Restorative Gifts
3. Lifestyle Gifts
4. Revelation Gifts
5. Directing Gifts
6. Guiding or Communication Gifts
7. Creative Gifts

To fully understand the spiritual gifts, I encourage you to study the supporting scriptures that are listed for each gift.

1. NURTURING GIFTS

ENCOURAGEMENT OR EXHORTATION

Attributes:

- Positive and optimistic – likes to converse and develop relationships.
- Exhorts and acknowledges others - they verbally encourage the wavering, the troubled or the discouraged.
- Known for sending thank-you cards and perfect greeting cards, always including a personal message that uplifts the recipient.
- Listening to people's struggles, they prescribe steps of action to aid personal growth.
- Are natural counselors - ministering words of comfort, consolation and challenge to others in such a way that they are strengthened, helped, nurtured, renewed and healed. If counselee doesn't follow their advice, they sense timing may not be good and will not push.
- They see potential in others and encourage them to become all they were created to be.
- They are quick to fix wrongs and reconcile strained relationships.
- They like to use personal illustrations when relating to others.
- Are able to inspire, motivate, strengthen, affirm, and be present with others, so they feel better equipped to meet life's challenges with confidence.
- They are trustworthy - people confide and share their innermost thoughts and feelings with them.
- Good at keeping conversations confidential.

They are a conduit for:

Ministering words of comfort, consolation, encouragement, and counsel. They see the potential in others and bringing out the best in people.

Supporting Scriptures:

Luke 3:18; Acts 11:23; Acts 14:21-22; Acts 20:1-2; Romans 12:6-8; 1 Thessalonians 2:11-12; Hebrews 3:13; Hebrews 10:25

Helps or Assistance

Attributes:

- Assisting, helping, and supporting other's in reaching their goals, and achieving their vision.
- Cheerfully performing supporting tasks (sometimes of a menial nature), for individuals or groups.
- Having an eye for details - anticipates needs and finds creative ways of making things happen.
- More interested in meeting the needs of others than their own.
- Needs to have direct contact with the person they are helping as they are more committed to the person than the task at hand.
- Can be bold and unafraid of taking authority; but they don't necessarily like taking the lead. They prefer to stay in the background joyfully helping.
- They are the wind beneath the wings of any leader, enabling them to accomplish goals that would not have been possible without their help.
- When they can't see the difference their help is making, they get discouraged.
- They have a hard time saying "No."
- Needs regular appreciation and praise.
- Enjoys working on short-term goals.

They are a conduit for:

Supporting and enabling others to serve more effectively.

Supporting Scriptures:

Mark 15:40-41; Luke 8:2-3; Acts 9:36; Romans 16:1-2; 1 Corinthians 12:28; 1 Timothy 5:10; 2 Timothy 1:16-18

Hospitality

Attributes:

- They focus on guests, and their needs.
- Can sense when someone feels out of place or uncomfortable and will purposefully initiate a conversation with them.
- Enjoys making people feel safe, welcomed and included - helps new people become a part of the group.
- They offer guests acceptance and a listening ear.
- Opens their home willingly and cheerfully to offer lodging, food, and fellowship.
- Likes it when people drop by and are not overly concerned if their home is not spotless.
- First to help host a visitor or take someone in that needs a place to stay and doesn't mind if they stay for an extended period.
- Has a warm and inviting home and is always friendly towards their guests.
- Always prepared to provide food or a beverage at a moment's notice. Will always make room at the table for extra guests.
- Enjoys hosting dinners, gatherings and social events and does so successfully.
- Great greeters for any function because they enjoy making guests feel welcomed.
- Enjoys visitors in their home, even when they don't know them well.
- Offers rides home or to appointments.

They are a conduit for:

Hospitality and making people feel welcomed, cared for, and included.

Supporting Scriptures:

Genesis 18:1-8; 2 Kings 4:8-10; Luke 10:38; Luke 24:28-29; Acts 16:14-15; Acts 28:7; Romans 12:13; Romans 16:23; Hebrews 13:2; 1 Peter 4:9

MERCY OR COMPASSION

Attributes:

- Able to love the unlovable without judgment.
- Identifies with those who suffer or are rejected by society - Feels the need to "be there" for them.
- Can quickly detect when someone is not doing well and is able to connect with the lonely, needy, oppressed, and less fortunate. Loves easing their burdens so they can relax, find rest, or smile again.
- Vulnerable and sensitive.
- Trustworthy but can also be too trusting.
- Feels genuine empathy and compassion for individuals challenged with physical, mental, or emotional problems and works to alleviate their distress.
- Ruled by their heart rather than their head. Feelings are more important to them than logic.
- Natural burden bearers, carrying the problems and worries of others in their heart. They are happy with those who are happy and weep with those who weep.
- Sees the dignity in people who are struggling with their circumstances.
- Devotes time and energy to work with the less fortunate, the homeless, the dying, people with AIDS, those in prison, the sick, the marginalized or the poor. Others are involved in animal rescue and care, or a cause to sustain the environment.
- They do well in ministries involving visiting hospitals, retirement homes, prisons, shut-ins or animal care and rescue.

They are a conduit for:

Responding to the emotional, and spiritual needs of others by showing them love, mercy, acceptance, and compassion.

Supporting Scriptures:

Isaiah 58:5-10; Micah 6:8; Matthew 5:7; Matthew 20:29-34; Matthew 25:34-40; Mark 9:41; Luke 10:30-37; John 8:3-11; Acts 9:36; Acts 11:28-30; Acts 16:33-34; Romans 12:8

2. RESTORATIVE GIFTS

HEALING

Attributes:

- Serves as human intermediaries through whom God restores health and well-being even when the medical system indicates it is not likely.
- Having compassion toward the sick and praying for them regularly.
- Their care has caused remarkable improvement in a person's physical, mental or emotional health.
- Uses prayer and conventional or alternative methods to treat people's physical ailments successfully.
- Using this gift may or may not require direct contact with the person who is ill.
- They may experience bodily heat, tingling hands, or a strong sense of God's presence when they pray or provide care for someone who is ill, as healing energy moves through them to the person they are helping.
- Feeling energized when they see improvement in sick or injured people under their care.
- Once this gift becomes known, the word spreads.
- This gift may not always involve a cure, for example, a hospice nurse with this gift may bring comfort and emotional healing while their patients still die.
- They understand that healing only occurs within the limits of God's will and timing. They trust and have faith that God can and will heal some and are not discouraged when he chooses not to.
- They recognize that doctors and medicine are often vehicles that God uses to bring about healing in a person.

They are a conduit for:

Physical or psychological healing.

Supporting Scriptures:

2 Kings 5:9-16; Matthew 20:29-34; Luke 9:1-2; Acts 3:1-8; Acts 5:12-16; Acts 8:4-8; Acts 9:32-35; Acts 14:8-10; Acts 20:7-12; Acts 28:7-9; 1 Corinthians 12:8-9; 1 Corinthians 12:28; James 5:13-16

INTERCESSORY PRAYER

Attributes:

- Feeling compelled to pray for a particular person, situation or request.
- Sometimes God wakes them up in the middle of the night to pray, and things happen when they do.
- They pray for extended periods of time on a regular basis. They know how long to pray and when they can stop. They may pray for several hours or days as God prompts them.
- They pray knowing the best outcome will happen.
- They view prayer as a genuine conversation with the Almighty God.
- God frequently speaks to them and they recognize His voice.
- They don't need to know the person they pray for and often pray for people they have never met.
- They see frequent and specific answers to their prayers and have a much greater occurrence of specific answers to prayer than most Christians.
- People often call on them to pray when they are facing difficult situations or decisions. It's a private ministry, not a public one – they should never be put in charge of a prayer group, etc.
- They use prayer to affect the external world.
- They pray without ceasing.
- People with this gift embrace the quote that says it best, 'Why worry when you can pray?'

110

They are a conduit for:

Miracles and change through prayer.

Supporting Scriptures:

Luke 22:41-44; Acts 12:12; Romans 8:26-27; 2 Corinthians 1:8-11; Ephesians 6:18; Colossians 1:9-12; Colossians 4:12-13; 1 Thessalonians 3:10; 1 Timothy 2:1-2

3. LIFESTYLE GIFTS

Celibacy or Singleness

Attributes: Mike

- Friendship is their most significant relationship. They usually have two or three good friends.
- They are single by choice, not circumstance and they love it.
- They live joyfully without the need for one intimate partner or spouse. They don't feel like they have to get married or pursue a committed romantic relationship.
- Not inclined to mate or procreate - have little difficulty controlling their sexual desires and don't suffer undue sexual temptations.
- Have undivided devotion and concern for the Lord's affairs – how they can please the Lord.
- Devoted to the Lord in both body and spirit.
- They like being mobile and unattached - the freedom allows them to be available to serve without distraction and be spiritually fruitful without the demands and responsibility of a family.
- They often feel judged and pressured by others to find a partner - it may be a mother telling them to find someone, settle down and marry; or it could be other couples. Because of this, they may question their choice to be single.
- Their career fulfills them, and they prefer it to marriage and family life.

- They like the freedom to control their own time without limitations.
- The gift of celibacy is a specific calling. It's not the same as being single, due to displaying a lousy personality or commitment issues.

They are a conduit for:

Available service anywhere God takes them.

Supporting Scriptures:

Matthew 19:10-12; 1 Corinthians 7:7-8; 1 Corinthians 7:32-35

X Faith - Trust

Attributes:

- Mountain-moving faith and courage - they have believed and have witnessed God do the impossible.
- They have an unusual measure of trust in the Holy Spirit's power.
- Deeply connected to God and have a constant dialogue with him.
- They act, in spite of the unknown – they have taken risks and leaps of faith in their life while being sure of God's love and power to provide.
- Thriving in and having faith in difficult situations that make others anxious or fearful, they can often shock other people with their confidence.
- Have few concerns - trusting and believing that everything occurs for a reason. They know that everything will work out just as it should.
- They have peace in situations where they have to rely on God's supply.
- When they make up their mind to trust and take action, nothing will stop them – they feel the fear and do it anyways.
- They don't seem to worry about details of the future, funds in the bank, retirement, or pension plans. They take God at His Word and put the full weight of their lives in His hands.
- They have unshakable confidence in the midst of crisis. They trust that God is Sovereign and He is good.
- They accept what is, without feeling like they have to make things happen.

They are a conduit for:

Courage and faith to bring the seemingly impossible to fruition.

Supporting Scriptures:

Malachi 3:10; Mark 5:27-29; Mark 12:41-44; Luke 7:1-10; Acts 27:21-25; Romans 4:18-21; 1 Corinthians 12:8-9; 2 Corinthians 8:1-15; James 5:14-16; Hebrews 11:1-40

Missionary or Apostleship ✕

The Greek word for Missionary or Apostle means "sent one." Literally one sent with authority, or as an ambassador or representative.

Attributes:

- They seek out opportunities to work with minorities and people of different language cultures or origins.
- As ambassadors or representatives of God's Gospel, they have a stronger than average desire to be a part of the fulfillment of the Great Commission around the world.
- They often become fluent in other languages to support those in different cultures.
- They find it easy and exciting to adjust to a different culture or community.
- People in other cultures are comfortable around them and embrace them easily.
- They like to travel to other countries to experience their cultures.
- They find it energizing and satisfying to connect directly with people different than themselves.
- They enjoy spending their time researching and learning about other cultures.
- They are a channel of God's love and provision among people of a culture other than their own.
- They might not have to travel to share this gift – they may be able to integrate into the diversity in their local area, through First Nations or embracing ethnic communities, such as Greek, Italian, Philippine, etc.

- They plant new ministries and churches in challenging environments where the gospel is currently not preached and then may oversee the expansion of these churches.
- This gift often pairs with the use of other gifts such as: Teaching, Mercy, Evangelism, Healing, Hospitality, etc., with the purpose of crossing cultural barriers.

They are a conduit for:

Bringing love, and the gospel message to other cultures.

Supporting Scriptures:

Matthew 28:16-20; Acts 1:8; Acts 8:4; Acts 9:15; Acts 13:1-4; Romans 10:15; 1 Corinthians 9:19-23; 1 Corinthians 12:28; Ephesians 3:6-8; Ephesians 4:11-13

VoluNTARY PoVERTY

Attributes:

- They choose simplicity, renouncing material comfort to adopt a personal lifestyle parallel to those living at the poverty level, in order to serve more effectively.
- They don't need to fill life with materialistic things and are happy to go without luxuries.
- Too many choices can overwhelm them.
- Living a simple lifestyle is an exciting challenge for them.
- They dislike clutter and don't have an excess of anything. They only have what is needed and used.
- They find joy and peace in a simple lifestyle. They dress, eat and live simply, by choice. External appearances are not important to them.
- People in less fortunate circumstances relate to them and feel comfortable with them.

- This gift has nothing to do with their financial state - they could have more things and afford luxuries but opt not to. They chose this lifestyle to identify with the materially poor.
- They don't fit comfortably in a materialistic culture and do not need to "Keep up with the Jones."
- People with this gift often cause others to examine their lifestyles and make connections that they don't require materialistic things to be happy.
- When someone gives them something beautiful, they might enjoy it briefly, later passing it on to someone else for their enjoyment.

They are a conduit for:

Bringing love and the gospel message to the poor and less fortunate by accepting, serving, and relating to them.

Supporting Scriptures:

Matthew 6:19-33; Luke 9:57-58; Acts 2:44-45; Acts 4:34-37; 1 Corinthians 13:1-3; 2 Corinthians 6:10; 2 Corinthians 8:9; 1 Timothy 6:6-10

4. REVELATION GIFTS

DISCERNMENT - DISTINGUISHING BETWEEN SPIRITS

Attributes:

- Discernment is a rare gift, often held by the spiritually mature.
- They quickly perceive divine or demonic presences in people, places, or things.
- This gift is not the same as standard human intuition. They obtain this special spiritual direction and understanding from God.
- They are often frank and outspoken with strong convictions to share what they are sensing.
- They view everything spiritual as black or white with very little gray.

- They can promptly and accurately sense the quality of someone's underlying intentions and motives, whether it's good or evil, right or wrong.
- They detect when something needs to be addressed.
- They recognize when a person is lying, distorting the truth, or communicating errors in teaching.
- They are able to identify the character of individuals or groups and can detect phoniness before it is evident to other people.
- Being sensitive to the spirit world, they can accurately tell if a person, or situation, is influenced by an evil or oppressive spirit or entity. Their knowingness on this is likely immediate and complete.
- They can easily help others see their blind spots.
- This gift is not meant to be used to criticize or judge; but to point others to a closer relationship with Christ.

They are a conduit for:

Understanding the non-physical realm; sensing good and evil, truth or lies, rights or wrongs.

Supporting Scriptures:

Matthew 16:21-23; Acts 5:1-11; Acts 16:16-18; 1 Corinthians 12:8-10; Hebrews 5:13-14; 1 John 4:1-6

Knowledge

Attributes:

- They have an unquenchable thirst for knowledge; spending countless hours researching or studying topics that are meaningful to them.
- Lifelong learners - seeking truth and facts in all matters.
- Usually well-versed in the scriptures; they like to help others distinguish important scriptural facts.
- They discover, accumulate, analyze, and clarify information because they are interested in ideas and solving problems.

- They ask questions to understand how people and the universe work at the most fundamental levels.
- They enjoy discovering new truths for themselves, through reading or observing situations firsthand.
- Once they acquire knowledge, they feel compelled to share what they have discovered and learned and are able to retain and communicate the truth effectively.
- Their creative, original, or groundbreaking intellectual work and efforts have resulted in both new discoveries and clarity in areas of importance.
- People seek their help when they need to understand complicated ideas and principles.
- They are at home in a book or studying, always have more than one book on the go and rarely part with their books.
- Those with this gift may have a low need for people, as they find themselves lost in their pursuit of learning.
- Instead of being caught up in emotions, events, and details, they prefer to focus on big-picture realities like human nature, ethics, natural law, scripture or other schools of thought.

They are a conduit for:

Discovering and sharing knowledge, ideas, direction, and solutions.

Supporting Scriptures:

1 Corinthians 12:8; 2 Corinthians 2:14; 2 Corinthians 11:6; Colossians 2:2-3

Wisdom

Attributes:

- This gift is for the spiritually mature.
- People will know them for their wise advice and wise speech.
- They meet impossible goals with their practical ideas, creativity, ingenuity, and innovation.

- They find and share practical solutions to complex personal or group problems. Their solutions change things for the better.
- They are perceptive and diplomatic and able to use skillful judgment. (Not the same as intuition).
- People seek their advice or counsel regarding challenging decisions or situations. They are able to guide individuals or the church through uncertainties or difficulties using their clear insight.
- This gift transforms hearts and lives.
- Wisdom is knowledge applied with common sense and understanding.
- When faced with important decisions, they feel the presence of God which gives them personal confidence.
- They have an excellent ability to apply spiritual truths to everyday life.
- They make good and correct decisions and judgments.

They are a conduit for:

Bringing wisdom to the world through sound advice and solutions to complex problems.

Supporting Scriptures:

Proverbs 4:5-8; Acts 6:3-10; 1 Corinthians 2:6-13; 1 Corinthians 12:8; *Colossians 1:9-10; Colossians 1:28; Colossians 2:1-3;* James 3:13-17; *2 Peter 3:15*

[handwritten annotation: a difference noted]

[handwritten annotation: v8 "Beware lest" ~ not after christ]

5. DIRECTING GIFTS

Administration

Attributes:

- These folks are often more task oriented than people oriented.
- They plan, coordinate, direct, supervise, and administer an already established goal or vision.

- They bring order to chaos and structure to the unstructured. With little effort, they can organize people, resources, and logistical details.
- They are effective planners, concerned with details and accuracy. They quickly break projects down into manageable tasks and accomplish them without wasted effort or confusion.
- They can give clear direction to others, without using persuasion to get the job done.
- Enjoyment comes from bearing the responsibility for the success of a particular project or task.
- They will create routine, structure, and systems; and are masters at streamlining procedures that maximize work efficiency.
- They respect authority, limits, rules, and laws and are fond of policies and procedures.
- There is a need to know how much authority they have, so they can respect those limits.
- They keep excellent notes, always have a "To Do" list and love checking off completed tasks.
- Responsible and reliable, they do what they say they will do.
- They thrive on the completion of things, be it a task, project or conversation.
- Loyal.
- They keep things in order, dislike dirt, clutter or disorganization and tend to be perfectionists.
- They will resume the leadership role if leadership does not exist.

They are a conduit for:

Getting things done, they bring planning, order, structure, routine, and completion to projects.

Supporting Scriptures:

Genesis 39:2-6; Genesis 41:46-49; Genesis 41:53-57; Exodus 18:17-23; 1 Corinthians 1:12:28; Corinthians 14:40; 1 Timothy 3:4-5; Titus 1:5

Giving

Attributes:

- Spontaneous and quick to volunteer where a need is identified; be it for a church work party, a worthwhile cause, or bringing a meal to a sick friend.
- Free and impulsive, they may be generous to a fault. Without restriction, they give of their money, possessions, time, energy, talents and love to make good things happen.
- Helpful to those in need, by providing money or material goods and directing where they will be of most benefit.
- Love to be personally involved in the giving, they desire to give to people, rather than projects.
- Belief in God is the source of their supply. They know He will take care of all their needs.
- Enjoyment comes from giving in secret, without claim or desire for credit. They give from the heart, with no ulterior motives.
- Hard working, with a tendency toward success, they have the ability to make large amounts of money or find the necessary resources through fundraising or other activities.
- Giving energizes them and they may feel called to philanthropy.
- Will sacrificially give to a cause they believe in.
- They like to give meaningful gifts.
- Mature givers resist pressured appeals and are not gullible or easily fooled.

They are a conduit for:

Contributing money or material goods to meet needs.

Supporting Scriptures:

Matthew 6:2-4; Mark 12:41-44; Acts 4:32-37; Acts 20:35; Romans 12:6-8; Romans 12:13; 1 Corinthians 13:3; 2 Corinthians 8:1-7; 2 Corinthians 9:2-15; Philippians 4:14-19

Leadership

Attributes:

- They are the inventors, innovators, founders, and creators among us.
- True visionaries who like to get involved in projects that stretch their imaginations and creativity. To keep their creative juices flowing, they require a lot of freedom to lead as they see fit.
- As natural born leaders who possess great zeal and enthusiasm, they can be enormously effective leading with little knowledge or skill in the specific area.
- They see the vision and quickly grasp the overall dimensions of a project or situation. When they are in charge, things run smoothly.
- They will articulate a vision with such excitement, energy and hope; that everyone gets on board, inspired, motivated and ready to participate in making things happen.
- They are able to build consensus, harness energy, and work with people to get important things done.
- When seizing opportunities or taking action, enjoyment is found in seeing how quickly they can accomplish what they need to do. They get bored easily.
- They pilot the ship – know the course and can steer the ship to stay on track. They tend to see potential problems in advance and can quickly and easily change direction. They are well equipped to lead in a crisis.
- Not happy staying with a project for long. Once something is running smoothly, they would rather turn it over to someone else and move on to new challenges.
- They are the most powerful motivational speakers in the world. When they speak, people listen and agree.
- They are constantly generating new ideas; but, can be weak at follow through. They live in a world of possibilities.
- Having an entrepreneurial spirit, they start groups or organizations and energize them when they are stagnant or disheartened, by suggesting ways to improve and better the situation.
- When they join a group, others naturally stand back and expect them to lead.

- Powerful mediators, negotiators, and problem solvers that thrive on demands, challenges, and change.
- Excellent at multi-tasking and juggling more than one project at any given time; they can keep them all separate and sorted out.
- They dislike paperwork and are not overly concerned with details. They do not enjoy routine or repetitive tasks, finding no challenge or interest in them.
- Delegating is a keyword for this gift. They are able to identify the gifts and talents of their team and delegate tasks accordingly. They are often more people oriented than task oriented.

They are a conduit for:

Vision, direction, and leading projects that improve the status-quo.

Supporting Scriptures:

Exodus 18:13-16; 2 Chronicles 1:7-12; Daniel 6:4; Acts 6:1-7; Romans 12:6-8; Hebrews: 13:7

SERVICE

Attributes:

- These are our worker bees [Marthas] of the world; they are empowered by doing. They are the hardest physical workers and tend to do more than what's asked of them. They may suffer burnout as a result.
- They like to see progress and prefer doing a job to talking about it. They are not good at delegating, because the joy for them comes from doing it themselves.
- They enjoy hands-on routine work and bring elbow grease and common sense to projects.
- Having an eye for detail, they identify what's needed and make use of available resources to help accomplish the task.

- Enjoyment is found in manual projects, jobs, and functions and they are quick to offer their physical help. Manual skill may include repairs, sewing, cooking, gardening, carpentry, electrical, etc.
- They are the essence of the 80/20 rule: 20% of the people do 80% of the work.
- When assisting, they may come across as impatient, pushy or bossy.
- They are helpful and do what needs to be done to bring the job to completion. As long as they are busy, they are happy.
- They are the backbone of any organization or structure; the great logistical person, the amazingly helpful gopher, the jack of all trades.
- They keep a list of what needs to be done, move fast, finish what they start and do it well. They can tend to be a perfectionist.
- They are known to keep things in perfect order.
- They are faithful and loyal.
- People with this gift are the cleanup crew when one is required.
- They are service-oriented and prefer taking orders to giving them. They can feel awkward when others want to serve them.

They are a conduit for:

Heartfelt service and getting things done.

Supporting Scriptures:

Genesis 39:6; Luke 22:24-27; John 12:26; Romans 12:6-7; 1 Corinthians 12:4-7; 1 Corinthians 16:15-16; Titus 3:14; 1 Peter 4:11; Revelations 2:19

6. GUIDING OR COMMUNICATION GIFTS

EVANGELISM

Attributes:

- They deliver a persuasive message that calls people to action.
- They bring the good news of the gospel and help people come to faith in Jesus.

- They passionately share a message or cause with others, who are inspired to embrace their belief.
- May feel compelled to start a ministry to improve society and people's lives.
- Can be bold, passionate, challenging, straightforward and influential.
- With clear intentions, they say what needs to be said to show someone right thinking.
- They can sense when someone is ready to accept Christ.
- When they share their faith and experience of God with non-believers, the hearers want to know more.
- They get frustrated when they feel alone in spreading the Word.
- They are drawn to groups that are unfamiliar with their belief because they desire to win them over.
- They are burdened for the lost and go out of their way to share the Truth.
- Generally, they have more success than other Christians in leading people to Christ.

They are a conduit for:

Calling people to believe in a cause or accept Jesus Christ as their Savior.

Supporting Scriptures:

Isaiah 52:7; Matthew 28:18-20; Acts 5:42; Acts 8:5-6; Acts 8:12; Acts 8:26-40; Acts 11:20-21; Acts 14:21; Romans 10:14-15; Ephesians 4:11-12; Ephesians 6:19-20; 2 Timothy 4:5

Prophesy

Attributes:

- Through their suffering, difficulties, and brokenness they have grown close to God. They view trials as opportunities for spiritual maturing and growth.
- They are the standard-bearers of Christianity – devoted to the truth, holiness, justice, and righteous standard of God's Word. They desire to get rid of their imperfections and be obedient to God at all cost.

- They believe that the Bible is a reliable basis for Truth, belief, action, and authority. They apply the Word of God to situations involving compromise, deception, dishonesty or evil. They desire to expose sin and restore relationships.
- Honest, upfront and candid; they tell it like it is. They tend to see issues as "right or wrong," "black or white," not "gray." They are not easily swayed by emotions.
- They receive messages and revelations not previously known and see things past, present, and future.
- Revelations that they feel compelled by God to deliver are received in the form of insights, dreams, visions or words.
- They perceive, pray about, proclaim and promote God's will. When they pass on the message they receive from God, it usually sparks worship, repentance or action. They expect an immediate response to the Truth they communicate.
- Their message will strengthen, comfort, encourage, guide, warn or rebuke. This gift edifies the church by making God's heart known.
- They may preach under the anointing of the Holy Spirit.
- Loyal to the Truth, even if it means cutting off relationships; They are willing to suffer for doing what is right in God's eyes.
- They know God's voice and have made accurate predictions that benefited or served others in a positive way.
- They test their revelations before speaking them.
- Others should weigh what a Prophet says against the scriptures and interpret the message accordingly.

They are a conduit for:

Predictions, warning, correction, restoration, and guidance.

Supporting Scriptures:

Deuteronomy 18:18-22; Luke 7:26-28; Acts 11:27-30; Acts 15:32-33; Acts 21:9-11; Romans 12:6; 1 Corinthians 12:7-11; 1 Corinthians 12:28; 1 Corinthians 14:1-5; 1 Corinthians 14:24-25; 1 Corinthians 14:29-33; Ephesians 4:11-14; 2 Peter 1:19-21

Shepherding or Pastoring

Attributes:

- They shepherd their flock by feeding, tending, and protecting them. They represent the heart of God and care for the Church.
- They preach the Word, correct, rebuke and encourage others with great patience and careful instruction.
- They accurately perceive when someone has to be boldly challenged about their spiritual, moral, or ethical behavior and will encourage them to take decisive action. They see through people's excuses and stories.
- They provide guidance and direction that nurtures relationships and promotes spiritual growth. They show people what's lacking spiritually in their lives and encourage and empower them to serve Christ and others.
- They boldly share their experiences of God to stimulate the spiritual life in others.
- People feel comfortable in their presence and seek their spiritual guidance.
- They may feel compelled to start a ministry through which they can improve society and people's lives.
- They sacrifice time and resources to support other people and build them up in their faith.
- They assume personal responsibility for the spiritual well-being of a particular group, sharing in their failures and successes.
- They care for the spiritually wounded and nurse them back to health.
- They bring others closer to God by how they live their life. They love the Gospel of Jesus Christ and put it at the center of their life and ministry.
- They want to know everyone personally in the groups they lead. They have a need for long-term relationships.
- They don't seek fame and recognition for themselves.
- They teach God's Word and are effective at restoring people to the Christian community or bringing them to know Jesus as their Lord and Savior.

They are a conduit for:

Biblical living and thinking, meeting needs, inspiring and nurturing spiritual growth, and helping people find Christ as their Savior.

Supporting Scriptures:

Jeremiah 3:15; Jeremiah 23:1-4; Ezekiel 34:1-16; John 10:1-18; Acts 20: 20-21; Acts 20:28; Romans 10:14-15; Ephesians 4:11-13; 1 Thessalonians 2:6-12; 1 Timothy 3:1-7; 1 Timothy 4:11-16; 1 Timothy 5:17; 2 Timothy 4:1-2; 1 Peter 5:2-4

Teaching

Attributes:

- They develop materials or learning opportunities to give people access to new knowledge or skills.
- They easily organize vast amounts of information and make it simple and easy to communicate, understand and remember.
- They love to study and research to learn new truths. Teachers believe the Truth has the intrinsic power to produce a change in people or situations. They accept without question that, "You will know the truth and the truth will set you free." John 8:32.
- They speak the Truth in love.
- Have a questioning mind, they ask: who, what, when, where, why and how come. They must guard themselves against skepticism as God moves.
- They can be more concerned with facts than feelings and tend to be more objective than subjective.
- They are systematic and logical presenters.
- They are clear thinkers.
- They adjust their content and delivery methods to meet the learning needs of a pupil or group. diplomacy
- They get energized when they teach information and skills that have a life-changing impact.
- They may use personal anecdotes to enhance a point.
- They enjoy words and see them as building blocks for communication. They develop and use an extensive vocabulary and are sticklers for proper grammar and correct spelling.

- They often sit in a course and think about how they can teach it better.
- They communicate Biblical truths to others and see resulting changes in knowledge, attitudes, values, or conduct.

They are a conduit for:

Presenting information that will help others grow and learn.

Supporting Scriptures:

Matthew 7:28-29; Matthew 28:19-20; Acts 18:24-28; Romans 12:6-7; 1 Corinthians 12:28; Ephesians 4:11-12; 1 Timothy 4:11-14; 1 Timothy 5:17; Hebrews 5:12-14; James 3:1

7. CREATIVE GIFTS

CraftsmanShip

Attributes:

- Visual and artistic, they have a creative mind and are very imaginative and innovative.
- They enjoy working with their hands. They find it profoundly satisfying to fix or create things.
- They have numerous vehicles of expression and are creative with material things: paint, clay, wood, food, plants, clothes, metal, etc.
- They often see how things run and operate and can fix them if needed. They are great at taking things apart and putting them back together.
- They desire to make things and can visualize how something will look before they create it.
- They love sharing what they create with others.
- Their creations inspire others.
- What others consider junk, they often treasure.
- They like building things from scratch.

Craftsmen are artistic and may do any of the following:

- o Living arts
- o Cooking
- o Sewing
- o Crafts
- o Decorating
- o Flower arranging
- o Interior design
- o Construction
- o Landscaping
- o Sculpting
- o Pottery
- o Drawing
- o Painting
- o Woodworking
- o Mechanics
- o Electronic or other repairs
- o Photography
- o And the list goes on and on

rough carpenter

They are a conduit for:

Bringing more creativity, beauty, and functionality to the world.

Supporting Scriptures:

Exodus 28:3-4; Exodus 31:1-11; Exodus 35:10; Exodus 35:30-35; Exodus 36:1; 2 Samuel 5:11; 1 Kings 7:13-14; 2 Chronicles 2:14; Proverbs 31-24; Ezekiel 27:4-11; Acts 18:3

Music

Attributes:

- Music is their primary form of artistic expression.
- They remember lyrics and tunes.

- They write or perform music for the delight of others.
- People are engaged and moved by the music they've performed and feel joyous, roused, and inspired.
- This gift manifests itself through arranging, composing, directing, producing, teaching or performing voice or instrumentation.
- They enjoy music and will often hum or sing along.
- This gift often shows up at an early age without training. They may have taught themselves to play a musical instrument.
- Their music can heal hurt and pain.
- They create a mood and enhance people's experiences in any situation; be it at an event, church, wedding, or a funeral, etc.
- Music can be a profound act of worship, petition, and praise.
- Whole music scores can appear complete in their mind along with the sound each music score would make.

They are a conduit for:

Vocal or instrumental music to evoke praise, worship, reflection, and celebration.

Supporting Scriptures:

1 Samuel 16:14-23; 1 Chronicles 15:16; 2 Chronicles 35:25; Psalm 32:11; Psalm 33:1-3; Psalm 95:1-2; Psalm 96:1-2; Psalm 100:1-2; Psalm 147:1; Psalm 147:7; Psalm 149:1; Psalm 149:3; Psalm 150; Mark 14:26; 1 Corinthians 14:26; Ephesians 5:19-20; Colossians 3:16

Writing

Attributes:

- They lose track of time when they write.
- Writing is their passion and an essential source of nourishment for their life.
- They enjoy putting ideas, thoughts and feelings down on paper.
- They process their experiences and express emotions through writing and may love to journal.

- They are deeply moved by the beauty, wit, and expressiveness of the written word. The magic and power of words hold a fascination and delight for them.
- They yearn to write a book, article, journal, etc.
- People appreciate their writing.
- They use words to create works of truth or beauty, to inspire, persuade, enlighten, shake people up, or stimulate the imagination.
- They turn to writing when they need to solve a problem, reach out to someone, explore an idea, or respond to a situation.
- With ease, they put what they've conceived into clear, useful and beautiful words.

They are a conduit for:

Relaying truth, beauty, or wit through the written word.

Supporting Scriptures:

Exodus 34:27; Isaiah 30:8; Habakkuk 2:2; Luke 1:1-3; Romans 15:4; Philippians 3:1; 1 Timothy 3:14-15; 1 John 2:12-14; Jude 3

All books of the bible were written by people who had the gift of writing.

ADDITIONAL GIFTS

Working of Miracles or Miraculous Powers

Many feel that the Working of Miracles gift is the same as the Healing gift. However, in *1 Corinthians 12:28*, they are listed as two separate gifts.

The Working of Miracles gift is a supernatural ability to serve others as a channel of God's miracle-working power, with no boundaries or limitations. This gift encompasses more than physical healings, with supernatural events that bring glory to God. The gift manifests itself through the supernatural intervention of God into specific circumstances that will change the perceived natural outcome. God notably worked miracles through Moses, his Apostles, and others that altered a person, place, or thing. The supernatural miracles God performed through these Biblical characters changed the ordinary course of nature. The effects of this gift are the same today as they were in Biblical times.

In *John 14:12-14* Jesus said, *"I tell you the truth, anyone who has faith in Me will do what I have been doing. He will do even greater things than these, because I am going to the Father. And I will do whatever you ask in My name, so that the Son may bring glory to the Father. You may ask Me for anything in My name, and I will do it."*

Jesus fed 5,000 men with a couple of fish and five loaves of bread. He cleansed the lepers, healed the lame, the blind, the sick, and raised several people from the dead. Everywhere He went He freed people from evil spirits and cast out demons. He turned water into wine, calmed a storm, and withered a fig tree. According to Jesus, believers will do even greater things (*John 14:12*).

Many third-world countries report that God works miracles for them all the time. So why don't we see them in our culture? I believe the gift has been ignored by today's lukewarm church due to their lack of faith and close relationship with God. We are called to have a childlike faith in Matthew's gospel. Perhaps our education with its reasoning and logic stand in the way of having the 'childlike faith' that it takes to see God's supernatural miracles?

In third-world countries, those who God has blessed with the Working of Miracles gift understand that God is Sovereign, and they are sensitive to His presence and power through His Holy Spirit. They can cast out demons in Jesus' name and instantly deliver people from demonic oppression or heal those who are sick. They don't fear demons and take authority over them in Jesus' name. When miracles occur, they give glory to God for His mighty works. They don't rely on their knowledge and abilities but on God's power to do the impossible. They exercise their 'childlike faith.'

Wouldn't it be great to witness God perform miracles? This dark world needs miracles today. To see this gift come to life in our churches starts with each believer repenting of their unbelief, asking God to increase their faith, and change them from the inside out. Several scriptures in the Bible state that we need to die to self and live for God. In *Galatians 2:20 (ESV)* Paul says, *"I have been crucified with Christ. It is no longer I who live, but Christ who lives in me. And the life I now live, in the flesh, I live by faith in the Son of God, who loved me and gave himself for me."*

Many need healing, and many need to be set free from demons, evil spirits or demonic oppression today. They need to witness how supernatural God is and this will only happen when we start living and doing what God wants us to do. It's about total surrender, dying to self and living for Christ. The Bible says that believers are foreigners and strangers on earth. Our eternal home is elsewhere, a place that God is preparing for all the followers of Jesus Christ. With that in mind, we need to focus on God's will, not our own. Rev 9:6 - our true interest is beyond the grave, not this world. The alternative isn't pretty.

Please join me in praying for the revival of this gift in today's modern church. Pray that the church will put away its programs and business-like etiquette and allow the Holy Spirit to have its way. It's time to have God brighten our dimmed lights so we can shine in this world. It's time to fall in love with Jesus and the work that He completed on the cross, taking away our sin and unrighteousness and replacing it with His righteousness. It's time to pray, study and meditate on God's Word. And above all else, it's time to put our selfish ambitions aside to win souls for His eternal Kingdom because time is running out! Rev 9:6 Die now while you can

Supporting Scriptures:

DELIVERANCE - *Matthew 12:22; Mark 3:14-15; Mark 6:13; Luke 10:17-20; Acts 8:5-8; Acts16:16-18; Acts 19:11-20; Ephesians 6:10-12*

MIRACLES - *Acts 2:22; Acts 6:8; Acts 9:36-42; Acts 19:11; Acts 20:7-12; Romans 15:17-19; 1 Corinthians 12:10-12; 1 Corinthians 12:28; 2 Corinthians 12:12; Galatians 3:5*

TONGUES AND INTERPRETATION OF TONGUES

Speaking in Diverse Tongues and the Interpretation of Tongues are listed throughout the New Testament as gifts to be used in the church. However, because these gifts are controversial today, and many don't embrace them, I've left them out of the primary teaching material.

Perhaps the gifts of Tongues and Interpretation of Tongues are so confusing and misunderstood among believers because they, like all of the spiritual gifts, are unexplainable in natural terms. All gifts are supernatural. It is therefore advisable to trust God's revelation of His supernatural gifts as you study them in the Bible. The Bible indicates that the Holy Spirit imparts gifts to believers to equip them to serve others and glorify God. We are God's hands, feet, eyes, ears, and voice on this earth and therefore need to ask what God wants to accomplish through us? We are not to question why He has created the gifts. Our job is to trust His Word, and trust that we are all gifted with spiritual gifts like the Bible states.

Many believe that speaking in tongues is only a prayer-praise language where one speaks to God in a divinely anointed utterance, a language they don't know. However, God's Word states that there is also a "gift" of Tongues, and a "gift" of Interpretation of Tongues, just like there is a "gift" of Encouragement, Leadership, Knowledge, etc. As an example, many of us can encourage others. However, that doesn't mean we have the "gift" of Encouragement. This works the same with Speaking in Tongues – not everyone will have it as a "gift," but many may still speak in unknown tongues.

Tongues are a supernatural ability to speak an unlearned language and the Interpretation of Tongues is a supernatural ability to translate an unlearned language. The Bible states that when the gift of Tongues is used in a group setting, there must be an interpretation or else the one speaking in tongues should remain silent. Tongues used without an interpretation only edify the speaker. A message given in tongues that also has an interpretation is designed by God to edify, exhort, or comfort the Church through instruction, exhortation, or correction. As stated in *I Corinthians 14:22*, tongues are a sign, not for believers, but for unbelievers.

I like the Apostle Paul's words in *1 Corinthians 14:14-19 NLT* where he says, *"For if I pray in tongues, my spirit is praying, but I don't understand what I am saying. Well then, what shall I do? I will pray in the spirit, and I will also* *pray in words I understand. I will sing in the spirit, and I will also sing in words I understand. For if you praise God only in the spirit, how can those who don't understand you praise God along with you? How can they join you in giving thanks when they don't understand what you are saying? You will be giving thanks very well, but it won't strengthen the people who hear you. I thank God that I speak in tongues more than any of you. <u>But in a church meeting I would rather speak five understandable words to help others than ten thousand words in an unknown language.</u>"*

We need to allow God to flow through the gifts He has imparted to all believers, as He sees fit. We must be sure that we are acting on God's prompting not our own. May we always be concerned about glorifying His name and doing His will.

Supporting Scriptures:

Mark 16:17; Acts 2:1-13; Acts 10:44-46; Acts 19:1-7; Romans 8:26-27; 1 Corinthians 12:10-30; 1 Corinthians 13:1; 1 Corinthians 14:1-28; 1 Corinthians 14:39

Chapter 14

✦

Affirming Your Gift Results

TESTING OUT YOUR GIFTS

- Involve others that know you well and ask for their insights and what they think you are gifted at doing – get affirmation. People will recognize the presence of a gift in you.
- Try out your gifts to see if they are a good fit. A spiritual gift is effortless to perform, feels natural, comfortable, and will always leave you feeling energized, full of joy, peace, creativity, and fulfillment. If you don't experience this, it's likely not a gift but a learned trait. This process may take some time to sort out but be patient because it is well worth it.
- You'll be effective and successful with the results you want to accomplish.

GIFTS PRODUCE RESULTS

Your gifts will manifest in results. Examples:

- Leadership – people will willingly follow your initiative and vision
- Teaching – people will learn
- Healing – people will get well
- Hospitality – people will feel welcomed and included
- Encouragement – people will feel exhorted and built up
- Prophesy – people will repent and make positive changes

PART VII

Spiritual Gifts Are Important, But Love Is More Critical

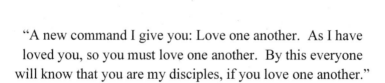

"A new command I give you: Love one another. As I have loved you, so you must love one another. By this everyone will know that you are my disciples, if you love one another."
John 13:34-35

CHAPTER 15

---✦---

THE GREATEST COMMANDMENTS ARE TO LOVE GOD AND ONE ANOTHER

LOVE CONQUERS ALL

When asked, *"Teacher, which is the greatest commandment in the Law?"* Jesus replied, *"Love the Lord your God with all your heart and with all your soul and with all your mind. This is the first and the greatest commandment. And the second is like it: 'Love your neighbor as yourself.'" (Matthew 22:36-40)*

We all want to be accepted and loved for who we are. Some of us are good at loving ourselves, we have healthy boundaries, take good care of our physical, emotional and spiritual health, yet we have a difficult time loving other people. Humans struggle with love because it's where the enemy, the devil, likes to attack us. Satan knows that God created us with different gifts so we would work together to bring His love to the world and bring strength and unity to the church body. Because Satan wants to destroy anything good, he works overtime to divide Christians and create dissension amongst them due to their characteristic differences.

I believe people struggle with self-esteem and self-confidence because they don't know who they are in Christ Jesus; how perfect, gifted, and capable they are in His sight. They may have had words spoken over them by family or friends that are a lie because that's what the devil encourages. *John 10:10* reads,

"The thief (the devil) comes only to steal and kill and destroy," the verse continues with Jesus saying, *"I have come that they may have life, and have it to the full."* That's the difference; the devil wants to destroy us, and Jesus wants to give us a fulfilling life. Don't believe the devil's defeating words about you, don't let him have victory in your life! Jesus' love, when He defeated the enemy on the cross, conquered all, and He is the reason we are capable of giving and receiving love. Rest in the love of Jesus today; His love abides in you, give it away whenever possible because love is the most powerful force on earth.

Love is more important than all the spiritual gifts exercised in the church body. Great faith, acts of dedication or sacrifice, and miracle-working power produce very little without love. Love makes our actions and gifts useful. Although people have different gifts, love is available to everyone.

Our society confuses love and lust. Unlike lust, God's kind of love is directed outward toward others, not inward toward ourselves. It is utterly unselfish. This kind of love goes against our natural inclinations. It is possible to practice this love only if God helps us set aside our own desires and instincts so that we can give love while expecting nothing in return. Thus, the more we become like Christ, the more love we will show to others.

If we love someone the way Christ loves us, we will be willing to forgive. If we have experienced God's grace, we will want to pass it on to others. And remember, grace is undeserved favor. By giving an enemy a drink, we're not excusing his misdeeds. We're recognizing him, forgiving him, and loving him in spite of his sins – just as Christ did for us.

Love is the greatest of all human qualities, and it is an attribute of God himself *(1 John 4:8)*. Love involves unselfish service to others. To show it, gives evidence that you care. Faith is the foundation and content of God's message, hope is the attitude and focus, and love is the action. When faith and hope are in line, you are free to love completely because you understand how God loves.

Spiritual gifts are shared in *1 Corinthians, chapters 12, 13, and 14*. It's interesting to note that in the middle of these chapters, chapter 13 is the familiar "love chapter." Love is the number one commandment for all believers. We can seek after gifts, but our priority should be to strive to love ourselves and others.

Recipe for Real Love

The Bible's love chapter, *1 Corinthians 13* says:

- Love is patient
- Love is kind
- Love does not envy
- Love does not boast
- Love is not proud
- Love is not rude
- Love is not self-seeking
- Love is not easily angered
- Love keeps no record of wrongs
- Love does not delight in evil
- Love rejoices with the truth
- Love always protects
- Love always trusts
- Love always hopes
- Love always perseveres
- Love never fails
- Love is greater than faith and hope
- Love endures forever

Can you imagine how you would feel if you were loved by everyone this way? Wouldn't it bring out the best in you?

Action Steps for Sincere Love

Romans 12:9-21 says:

- Love must be sincere
- Hate what is evil; cling to what is good
- Be devoted to one another in brotherly love
- Honor one another above yourselves

Erika Larsson
AUTHOR, TRAINER, SPEAKER

RISING HIGHER – Four Steps to Finding and Living Your Purpose

WEEK 5 HOMEWORK

In the Rising Higher book read the following pages:

Pages 158-165

Pages 170-182

If you haven't completed your final Life's Purpose Statement, complete it before next week's session.

- Never be lacking in zeal, but keep your spiritual fervor serving the Lord
- Be joyful in hope
- Be patient in affliction
- Be faithful in prayer
- Share with God's people who are in need
- Practice hospitality
- Bless those who persecute you; bless and do not curse
- Rejoice with those who rejoice
- Mourn with those who mourn
- Live in harmony with one another
- Do not be proud; but, be willing to associate with people of low position
- Do not be conceited
- Do not repay anyone evil for evil
- Respect what is right in the eyes of men
- If it is possible, as far as it depends on you, live at peace with everyone
- Do not take revenge, but leave room for God's wrath, for it is written: "It is mine to avenge; I will repay," says the Lord
- If your enemy is hungry, feed him; if he is thirsty, give him something to drink – in doing this, you will heap burning coals on his head
- Do not be overcome by evil, but overcome evil with good

Do Everything in Love

We can be gifted and capable of performing great works, but without love it amounts to nothing. Take some quiet time to read and meditate on the following scriptures about love:

"If I speak in the tongues of men and of angels, but have not love, I am only a resounding gong or a clanging cymbal. If I have the gift of prophecy and can fathom all mysteries and all knowledge, and if I have a faith that can move mountains, but have not love, I am nothing. If I give all I possess to the poor and surrender my body to the flames, but have not love, I gain nothing." *(1 Corinthians 13:1-3)*

"Do everything in love." (1 Corinthians 16:14)

"Speaking the truth in love, we will in all things grow up into Him who is the Head, that is, Christ. From Him the whole body, joined and held together by every supporting ligament, grows and builds itself up in love, as each part does its work." (Ephesians 4:15-16)

"Above all, love each other deeply, because love covers over a multitude of sins." (1 Peter 4:8)

Be a Fruit Bearing Christian

Love is an automatic side effect of having a close relationship with God. When we spend time praying, worshiping, reading the Word of God and meditating on it, we see evidence of spiritual fruit in our lives. It's through our connection with the Almighty God that His attributes show up such as love, joy, peace, patience, kindness, goodness, faithfulness, gentleness and self-control, which are fruits of the Spirit listed in *Galatians 5:22-23*. The fruits of the Spirit in us, is what helps us to stand out in this dark world as a beacon of light. *"By their fruit you will recognize them." (Matthew 7:16)*

Spiritual gifts are significant, but love is far more critical. Let us start to consciously, *"Show proper respect to everyone: Love the brotherhood of believers, fear God, honor the King,"* as stated in *1 Peter 2:17*.

Chapter 16

---✦---

Be Still

GOD WANTS US TO BE STILL

As believers, we must realize that we have the life of Christ living in us by the Holy Spirit. *Acts 17:28,* says, *"In Him we live and move and have our being."* Yet, so many believers only focus on Christ in a Sunday church service. Christ is not a lifeless idol but an all-powerful living being who desires that we bring Him into every aspect of our daily lives. We will only experience Christ's life and His promise, *"I have come that they may have life, and have it to the full"* *(John 10:10),* working in and through us, when we spend intimate time with Him on a daily basis.

Psalm 46:10 says, *"Be still, and know that I am God."* We are rarely still today.

In our spare time do we text, surf the web and social media, watch TV, talk to friends or spend time with God? Does God have a lower priority in our life than other free time activities? To have the life we desire and deserve, we must give God the best part of our day, and the rest will fall into place.

The Bible promises for putting God first are incredible – anything else pales in comparison. If we are feeling weary, are enduring hardships, or wondering what this life is all about, we should spend time with God, like we would a best friend, and watch how our circumstances and contentment level improve.

Get into the habit of taking quiet time and being still with God every day – it's in the quietness that He speaks to us. Silence is a source of great strength. It's refreshing and gets rid of the noise in our head. On a daily basis, Jesus left to have His quiet time with God. If Jesus needed that time to talk to God, don't you think we need it?

PART VIII

Living A Purposeful Life

"For I know the plans I have for you," declares the LORD,
"plans to prosper you and not to harm you, plans to
give you hope and a future."
Jeremiah 29:11

Chapter 17

---✳---

Passion Is the Compass to Your Purpose

We have been doing quite a bit of reflecting and learning about how God has wired us. He loves us so much that He has given each of us a specific purpose here on earth. Let's think now about what that is.

YOUR LIFE MATTERS

- Are you living up to your potential?
- Do you feel unfulfilled and unsatisfied?
- Do fear and uncertainty bind you?
- Does life seem meaningless and empty?
- Do you know your life's purpose?

If you are stirred by the above questions or feel that your life is lacking in meaning, the next two chapters are designed to help you discover your passion and purpose so you can live the life God intended for you to live.

When God created you, He placed in you everything needed to fulfill your calling and purpose. He's given you the desire, ability, and has stirred your heart and filled it with passion. He's equipped you with the required gifts. He's given you the ideas, creativity, and specific areas in which you will shine. No dream is too big; no challenge is too great for Him to accomplish through you.

We keep trying to fix things in ourselves that are not broken. We need to stop comparing ourselves with others, trying to turn ourselves into the best version of somebody else. God created us the way we are, with the gifts we have, to fulfill our destiny. *Ephesians 2:10* reads, *"For we are God's handiwork, created in Christ Jesus to do good works, which God prepared in advance for us to do."*

When we are in Christ, no college degree or specialized qualifications are Acts necessary; only our availability and God will take care of the rest. Any sense of 4:13 self-reliance will serve as a roadblock, because it is in our weaknesses that God expresses His strength, and in our foolishness, that He expresses His wisdom.

People are rarely good at duties they don't enjoy doing. God knows that we are always motivated and happy when we do things we love to do. This is why His plan to use the gifts He has given us to bless others, while also energizing us is so beautiful. It's when we are not using our gifts, or our heart is not in what we are doing that we are easily discouraged, lose confidence in ourselves, and life becomes a constant struggle.

God wants us to use the gifts He's bestowed on us to serve Him passionately; not from a sense of duty. People who achieve noteworthy things are those who do it because of passion, not for money. Too often people waste their life in a job that doesn't fill them with enthusiasm or express their heart's desires. Their life goal is to work hard to accumulate financial wealth, which can be lost. This mindset robs them of the rewarding life God intended for them to have. Instead, we need to focus on using our gifts to produce eternal rewards that no one can take from us – that's the solution to a happy life. *Matthew 6:19-20 (ESV)* says, *"Do not lay up for yourselves treasures on earth, where moth and rust destroy and where thieves break in and steal, but lay up for yourselves treasures in heaven, where neither moth nor rust destroys and where thieves do not break in and steal."*

Aim for a life worth living by serving God in a way that expresses the passion in your heart. People who live passionate lives are contagious! God wants us to be contagious.

God is not just the starting point of your life; He is the source of it. God made you for a reason, and your life has profound meaning!

Take time to read, reflect, and meditate on the following scriptures about living a purposeful life:

"Do not neglect the gift of God within you." (1 Timothy 4:14)

"The heart of a man plans his way, but the Lord establishes his steps." (Proverbs 16:9 ESV)

"I urge you to live a life worthy of the calling you have received." (Ephesians 4:1b)

"Doing the will of God from the heart." (Ephesians 6:6b)

PASSION = PURPOSE

GREEK: Passion is a feeling of intense enthusiasm (entheos) which means "filled with God."

Passion is God within; it is the compass to our purpose. Our passion is our purpose!

The Bible tells us in *Proverbs 29:18 KJV, "Where there is no vision, the people perish."* Without passion and a dream, our purpose is limited and our life will seem meaningless.

QUALITIES TO HELP US IDENTIFY OUR PURPOSE

If we are passionate and enthusiastic about an issue or need in the world that we can't let go of or that we daydream about changing, it's most likely God trying to steer us towards our purpose. When something is our passion, we can't get enough of it. We read about it, study it, and never run out of ideas about it.

148

Below are some common qualities people have when they are identifying their passion:

- We have a vision (passion) of how an issue or need in the world could be different. This stirring, thought, dream, feeling, prompting or wish won't leave us alone. We can't dismiss it because it shows up again and again in our mind.
- The need (pain or frustration with what is) in our vision, tugs at our heart. We may see things on TV or in our community that instantly stir up pain and frustration for us, and we wish we could do something to change it.
- We desire to pursue our vision to serve others. It feels like it's our assignment.
- Ease, flow, and great joy accompany any work we do that resembles our vision/dream.
- We resist our vision because it feels too big, may upset current plans, is daunting, scary or inconvenient. Consider it may just be God-sized and is exactly what we should do.
- We don't have everything we need to pursue the vision. We justify that we can't do it because we don't have the right relationships, skills or resources required. Trust that we will gather those things as we take a step of faith, not before. God provides for what He decides.
- We are not yet who we need to be to complete our vision. We talk ourselves out of our calling by saying we lack the right education, charisma, courage, etc. to do it. Our callings are there to grow us. Step out in faith and experience God move in powerful ways, if it is meant to be.

OUT OF PAIN, BEAUTY IS BORN

Our passion often comes from the painful events and trials we've endured in life. God never wastes a hurt! He refines us in our fiery trials and builds our faith. When we go through a hurt, we have first-hand experience and understanding, and develop empathy for others going through similar situations. Our suffering helps us grow by cultivating discipline, patience, and endurance in us. Often our pain reveals God's purpose for our lives.

The pain we've suffered can become our ministry to others - this is called redemptive suffering – meaning we go through it for the benefit of others. This is what Jesus did. He didn't deserve to die on the cross; but, He went through the pain for our benefit so we can be forgiven of our sin and find a whole new life in Him.

Take time to read, reflect, and meditate on the following scriptures about suffering and trials:

"Consider it pure joy, my brothers, whenever you face trials of many kinds, because you know that the testing of your faith develops perseverance. Perseverance must finish its work so that you may be mature and complete, not lacking anything." (James 1:2-4)

"God comforts us in all our troubles so that we can comfort others." (2 Corinthians 1:4 NLT)

"See, I have refined you, though not as silver; I have tested you in the furnace of affliction. For My own sake, for My own sake, I do this." (Isaiah 48:10-11a)

"In all this you greatly rejoice, though now for a little while you may have had to suffer grief in all kinds of trials. These have come so that your faith – of greater worth than gold, which perishes even though refined by fire – may be proved genuine and may result in praise, glory and honor when Jesus Christ is revealed." (1 Peter 1:6-7)

"We rejoice in our sufferings, knowing that suffering produces endurance, and endurance produces character, and character produces hope." (Romans 5:3-4 ESV)

HOW GOD REFINES US IN OUR SUFFERING:

- Helps us get rid of sin in our lives and leads us to repentance
- Helps us deepen our commitment and our relationship with Christ

- Helps us depend on His grace
- Helps us develop compassion and empathy for others
- Helps us gain wisdom
- Helps us desire God's Truth
- Helps us learn to give thanks in all circumstances
- Helps us discipline our minds – learning to take our thoughts captive
- Helps us cultivate patience and endurance
- Helps us bond with other people who understand
- Helps strengthen our character
- Helps us develop discernment
- Helps us increase our faith and hope

Once we grasp the love, the value, and the lessons that our pain and suffering have brought us, we can say, "It was worth it!" It is then that God will use our story to bless others.

CALLINGS HAVE A THREE-FOLD PURPOSE

1. To bring light into this dark world
2. To grow us into a more expansive, mature, beautiful version of ourselves
3. To be God's hands and feet in the world

Saint Teresa of Avila said:

- Christ has no body now on earth but yours
- Yours are the eyes through which He sees where compassion is needed in this world
- Yours are the feet with which He walks to do good
- Yours are the hands through which He blesses the world

Chapter 18

Discovering Your Purpose

DISCOVERING YOUR PURPOSE EXERCISE

To help you clarify and identify your purpose, spend some time reflecting on the following questions before you answer them. Some people find it helpful to journal about each question to achieve clarity.

1. When in your life have you been the happiest? (as a child and as an adult)

2. What activities were your favorite in the past? What about now?

3. What activities make you lose track of time?

4. What have you done that made you truly proud of yourself?

5. What is it that makes you feel alive, energized, and fulfilled?

6. Who inspires you and what qualities do they possess? (Family, friends, authors, artists, leaders, etc. You may or may not know them personally).

7. What are you naturally good at? (skills, abilities, gifts, etc.)

8. What do people typically ask you for help with?

9. If you could teach anything you wanted, what would you teach?

10. What causes do you strongly connect with and believe in?

11. If you could relay a message that you're passionate about to a large audience, what would your message be and who would be in attendance listening?

12. If you could change or remove one thing in the world, what would it be? What would you replace it with? (Example: remove war and replace with peace, remove abuse and replace with total acceptance and love, remove poverty and replace with abundance).

PREPARING YOUR PURPOSE STATEMENT

When you have answered the above questions, prepare your life purpose statement by incorporating:

- Your personality/top gifts
- Your passion/purpose

Once you have identified your personality style, and your spiritual gift DNA and you know your passion, draw a picture of your future or create a collage and write your purpose statement on it. Read it on a consistent basis to remind yourself of who you were created to be. I call it my 'Rule of Life' statement.

PROVISION COMES AFTER WE STEP OUT IN FAITH

Taking the first step to follow our passion by serving others can be daunting, and downright scary. Reach deep within for faith. Ask God to lead you, and to open and close doors according to His purpose. When you're on the right track following your passion and purpose, you'll find open doors of opportunity. People will show up that can help you on your way. You'll see God's miraculous powers at work and before you know it, your doubts will dissipate, your insecurities and fears will vanish.

"And we know that in all things God works for the good of those who love Him, who have been called according to His purpose." (Romans 8:28)

CONFIDENCE COMES FROM OBEDIENCE

You may think (even after all we've discussed) that you have no special talent, that there is nothing special about you, and may question how God could use someone ordinary like you. Rest assured, you're not alone in your thinking. It's the devil's secret weapon to keep us thinking defeating thoughts. Don't conclude that the best you'll ever do is stand in the shadows of the people that God is using. You are chosen, and it is not in your power that the gifts operate but in the power of a risen Christ! We merely need to obey. God will show up!

Consider these words from *1 Corinthians 1:26-29, "Brothers and sisters, think of what you were when you were called. Not many of you were wise by human standards; not many were influential; not many were of noble birth. But God chose the foolish things of the world to shame the wise; God chose the weak things of the world to shame the strong. God chose the lowly things of this world and the despised things–and the things that are not–to nullify the things that are, so that no one may boast before Him."*

Anyone who's suffered abuse, tends to think they are too damaged to be used by God. Think again, because God loves broken vessels, they are precious to Him, and He restores them and does great work through them as they rely on Him. God is the Potter, we are the clay, and when we allow Him to mold us, He makes us into something beautiful and useful. *(Isaiah 64:8)*

Satan is clever and knows that negative and defeating thoughts make us feel unworthy. He loves to make us feel unqualified and to get us to compare ourselves to others. He'll do his best to convince us that we don't measure up to other people, so we should quit. The devil's goal is to kill our God-given vision, passion, and purpose, and he'll shower us with shame, guilt, and condemnation to halt us in our tracks. He'll use any trick he can, in hopes of stopping us from doing the right thing. We all go through this torment but need to learn that the only opinion that matters is God's. He decides our value and our future.   Jud. 4:9   5:1

When we live for God; trials, uncertainty, and struggles will happen, but we can trust He has our best interests in mind. He has the plan and knows what lies ahead. When we face obstacles, God knows the way around them no matter how difficult they look to us. Be assured that He will work everything out for our benefit and God's glory. All we need is faith, and that comes from hearing and knowing the Word of God *(Romans 10:17)*.

We should not allow our insecurities or shortcomings to dictate if, or how, we allow God to use us. To God, we are gifted and worthy! Look at the Bible characters that failed God. Judges 5   2 Ki 7:1 + 17

Even though Peter was a risk-taking hothead, God had a plan for him which Jesus revealed in *Matthew 16:18-19* where He said, *"You are Peter, and on this rock I will build my church, and the gates of Hades will not overcome it. I will give you the keys of the kingdom of heaven; whatever you bind on earth will be bound in heaven, and whatever you loose on earth will be loosed in heaven."* Peter walked and talked with Jesus, witnessed Him do miracles and healings, yet Peter denied knowing Jesus three times before the rooster crowed. Peter Jn 21: later repented of his sin, and Jesus restored him and used him to spread the 15 - 17 gospel message that added 3,000 people to the church in one day. Peter was a conduit of God's power. He healed the sick and preached the Good News to both Jews and Gentiles.

John the Baptist struggled or had humility with feelings of being unworthy. He said he was not worthy to stoop down to untie the straps of Jesus' sandals in *Mark 1:7*, yet God used him to announce the arrival of the Messiah, and later to baptize Jesus. Jesus said in *Matthew 11:11, "Among those born of women there has not risen anyone greater than John the Baptist."*

The Apostle Paul wrote half of the Bible's New Testament and was a well-known missionary and church planter, yet he was another person who questioned his worth. Paul said in one of his letters to the church in Corinth that he was the least of all the apostles. He felt unworthy of being called one of Jesus' Apostles because in his past, he persecuted God's church *(1 Corinthians 15:9)*, yet he was used mightily by God and gave his life for the cause of Christ.

Even though Paul persecuted Christians, Jesus had a plan for him and said in *Acts 9:15, "This man is my chosen instrument to carry my name before the Gentiles and their kings and before the people of Israel."*

As you can see from the above examples, it doesn't matter who we are or what we've done; God still has a plan for us and desires to flow through us. If we've made mistakes, mistreated others, lied, cheated, or anything else that we feel sorry about, repent of our wrongdoings because Jesus will forgive us. And if we're willing to make a difference through a life of service, God will use us. Everything is possible with God! Don't let your self-judgments stand in the way of allowing God to use your gifts to perform His transformational work in the world. In *2 Corinthians 12:9a*, Paul quotes what Jesus said to him, *"My grace is sufficient for you, for my power is made perfect in weakness."* In *2 Corinthians 12:9b-10*, Paul said, *"Therefore I will boast all the more gladly about my weaknesses, so that Christ's power may rest on me. That is why, for Christ's sake, I delight in weaknesses, in insults, in hardships, in persecutions, in difficulties. For when I am weak, then I am strong."*

We read in the Bible about water turned to wine, the sea parted so the Israelites could pass through on dry ground, numerous healings, and dead people raised to life. Often, we look at these miraculous events and think we have to produce them too, but it is not our responsibility. As a follower of Christ, our responsibility is to put our trust in Jesus, obey the promptings and instructions of the Holy Spirit and leave the results and consequences to God. In our flesh, we cannot make anything happen; to think so is foolishness. It is in our obedience and dependence on God and His miracle-working power, that He accomplishes what seems impossible through us. We are just the conduit through which He works.

Many Christians today have a casual attitude towards obedience to Christ and they have little trust in His miracle-working power, which inhibits the work of Christ in their lives. So often we feel apprehensive or fearful of stepping out in faith and obedience because we fear what others will think or say; but, we need to fully trust God because He will always generate results and boost our faith in the process!

Stephen Olford, author and evangelist, said, "God won't teach you anything new until your obedience to Him is up to date." This is a powerful and true statement!

Though we all feel unqualified and ordinary, phenomenal things will occur when we choose to surrender, step out in faith, and operate according to Christ's agenda, doing what He tells us, having full dependence on His power working through our weakness and inadequacies.

PART IX

Showing Kindness to the Poor and Needy

"Remove the heavy yoke of oppression.... Feed the hungry, and help those in trouble. Then your light will shine out from the darkness, and the darkness around you will be as bright as noon. The LORD will guide you continually, giving you water when you are dry and restoring your strength."
Isaiah 58:9-11 NLT

Chapter 19

---✦---

You Are Created to Serve Others

JESUS SAID THE WAY TO BE GREAT IS TO SERVE OTHERS

"The greatest among you will be your servant." (Matthew 23:11)

"Whoever wants to become great among you must be your servant, and whoever wants to be first must be a slave of all. For even the Son of Man did not come to be served, but to serve, and to give His life as a ransom for many." (Mark 10:43b-45)

"Each one should use whatever gift he has received to serve others." (1 Peter 4:10)

"Serve one another humbly in love." (Galatians 5:13b)

"If anyone wants to be first, he must be the very last, and the servant of all." (Mark 9:35)

ARE YOU WILLING TO SERVE?

God desires to flow through our gifts, but He won't force us to live a life of service to Him; it's our choice. Will you choose to be a conduit that He can

159

flow through? God is waiting to partner with us to make a difference in our communities and the world, but we have to surrender to His will and be willing to do what He asks us to do. If every believer in the world participated in making positive changes to help the needy and hurting, our impact would mend a lot of the brokenness we witness around us.

We have become an ungodly world, more concerned about our pleasures than God's will. *2 Timothy 3:1-5*, sounds like it was written to describe events going on today. It reads, *"But mark this: There will be terrible times in the last days. People will be lovers of themselves, lovers of money, boastful, proud, abusive, disobedient to their parents, ungrateful, unholy, without love, unforgiving, slanderous, without self-control, brutal, not lovers of the good, treacherous, rash, conceited, lovers of pleasure rather than lovers of God - having a form of godliness but denying its power."*

When people turned from their sin and complacency in the Old Testament, God instantly came to their rescue. We need to do the same today. We need to repent and ask God for help. We are called to be servants of God. Will we answer the call? *"Jesus Christ is the same yesterday and today and forever."* *(Hebrews 13:8)*

BE PART OF THE SOLUTION FOR OUR HURTING WORLD

God is a God of miracles, and the world needs miracles right now. Are we willing to seek God and ask Him what our part is in helping the poor, feeding the hungry or providing a home for a foster child? What role may we have in healing the sick, providing relief for a single mother, mentoring troubled youth, serving meals to the homeless, visiting the elderly, volunteering at a sex trafficking hotline, or raising funds to help support a non-profit organization? There is something each and every one of us can do to make a difference. Let's take action today! God wants to ignite our passion for helping to fix this broken world; He wants us to be part of the solution.

In *Matthew 25:35-36*, Jesus said, *"For I was hungry and you gave Me something to eat, I was thirsty and you gave Me something to drink, I was a stranger and you invited Me in, I needed clothes and you clothed Me, I was sick and you looked after Me, I was in prison and you came to visit Me."*

One of Mother Teresa's favorite scriptures, which she often quoted to support her ministry to the poor, is found in *Matthew 25:40*, where Jesus said, *"Truly I tell you, whatever you did for one of the least of these brothers and sisters of mine, you did for Me."*

Chapter 20

---- ✳ ----

Making a Difference

PRACTICAL WAYS TO SERVE OTHERS

Your willingness matters to God! You may be ready to participate in making a change but wonder where to start. I urge you to pray and let your passion and purpose be your guide. Do some exploring of problems and issues in your community, maybe search for non-profit organizations where you can help, or consider starting with some of the suggestions listed below:

- Help a single mom feel refreshed by taking her kids for a few hours
- Help a widow with her yard work or necessary repairs
- Befriend a war veteran or someone with a disability
- Bring dinner to a family who has suffered a recent tragedy
- Visit the elderly and consider taking them out into nature or for ice cream
- Bring groceries to a family in need or give them a food voucher
- Help at a local food bank or donate food to them
- Send a care package or a letter to overseas troops
- Help a senior or a single parent organize their house
- Help an elderly person with house cleaning
- Run errands for the elderly
- Pray with someone who has a need
- Spend time with a struggling teenager and do something fun with them

- Buy an outfit for a single mom
- Offer a ride to someone who has no car
- Make care packages to hand out to people asking for money
- Befriend an elderly person who is lonely – there is a great need in this area as many are lonely, especially those who live alone
- Donate clothes
- Get to know your neighbor by having them over for a meal
- Throw a birthday party for a child in an impoverished neighborhood
- Buy school supplies for a low-income family
- Bring food and beverages to a single person who is too sick to get out
- Bring flowers from your garden to someone who is sick or elderly
- Take someone's pet for a walk if they are ill or unable to do it themselves

If you have time for a greater commitment, consider these ideas:

- Raise funds for a cause you strongly believe in and connect with
- Become a mentor
- Hold a neighborhood food drive
- Arrange a team to help clean up your community, or a park
- Volunteer at a soup kitchen, a shelter for the homeless, youth center, etc.
- Share produce from your garden or fruit trees
- Prepare meals for an elderly person living alone
- Volunteer for Hospice, or visit people in jail, a nursing home, or hospital
- Donate your skills as a plumber, electrician, handyman, mechanic, hair-stylist, etc. to help someone who can't afford to hire help
- Adopt a foster child to keep them out of the human trafficking circle
- Become an honorary aunt or uncle to a foster child
- Hold a neighborhood coat drive in the early winter months
- Arrange fun activities for children of impoverished families
- Create an organization to fill a need
- Gather blankets from neighbors and deliver them to the homeless
- Teach free classes to youths like; photography, flower arranging, wood-working, mechanics, painting, drawing, cooking, outdoor survival, sewing, music, gardening, graphic design, etc.
- Start a movement that will have a positive impact in your community; like 'pay it forward,' 'random acts of kindness,' etc.

- Go on a mission trip to build homes for the less fortunate
- Start a coffee house with live music in your neighborhood where new residents or lonely people can gather to have fellowship

The possibilities are endless. It starts with every person looking into their hearts to see what calls to them; getting in touch with their God-given passion and taking action to make a difference. Find a need and fill it. When you open yourself up to serving by using your gifts, you'll be surprised at how many opportunities will show up. Remember, nothing is impossible with God. He parted the Red Sea, fed five thousand people with two fish and five loaves of bread, raised the dead, turned water into wine, healed the lepers. This is the same God whose Spirit lives inside you and empowers you. Your job is to be a willing conduit for God's power to flow through; you are His partner to help make this world a better place.

The Bible mentions helping the needy and poor over 300 times. When every believer chooses to participate to make a difference, and takes action, miracles will happen. Collectively, the Body of Christ can turn sorrows into joy, starting with you. Go and do what God is asking of you. You don't need to know the how, you just need to be obedient and trust that God will give you whatever you need to accomplish what He is asking of you. Start making a difference, one life at a time. Feeling sorry for those who suffer and shedding tears about it isn't enough. Taking action, is what's necessary.

"What good is it my brothers and sisters, if someone claims to have faith but has no deeds? Can such faith save them? Suppose a brother or a sister is without clothes and daily food. If one of you says to them, "Go in peace; keep warm and well fed," but does nothing about their physical needs, what good is it? In the same way faith by itself, if it is not accompanied by action, is dead." (James 2:14-17)

KINDNESS TO THE POOR AND NEEDY WILL BE REWARDED

The Bible has many promises for those who show kindness to the poor and needy. Take time to read, reflect, and meditate on the following scriptures:

164

"If anyone has material possessions and sees a brother or sister in need but has no pity on them, how can the love of God be in that person?" (1 John 3:17)

"Whoever oppresses the poor shows contempt for their Maker, but whoever is kind to the needy honors God." (Proverbs 14:31)

"Whoever is kind to the poor lends to the LORD, and He will reward them for what they have done." (Proverbs 19:17)

"Whoever shuts their ears to the cry of the poor will also cry out and not be answered." (Proverbs 21:13)

"Those who give to the poor will lack nothing, but those who close their eyes to them receive many curses." (Proverbs 28:27)

"Whoever sows sparingly will also reap sparingly, and whoever sows bountifully will also reap bountifully." (2 Corinthians 9:6 ESV)

"God is not unjust; He will not forget your work and the love you have shown Him as you have helped His people and continue to help them." (Hebrews 6:10)

PART X

Deepening Our Commitment

"Salvation is found in no one else, for there is no other name
under heaven given to men by which we must be saved."
Acts 4:12

Chapter 21

---✦---

Jesus Is the Way

FILLING THE VOID

We are created with a void, a spiritual vacuum.

God didn't design us to wander through life, continually wondering who we are, and why we're here. He sent Jesus into the world to bring us back to God, back to the relationship God intended for us to have with Him.

Humans are notoriously poor at knowing what will truly satisfy them; always seeking after purpose, meaning, happiness, fulfillment, and inner peace. In this pursuit they reach for power, fame, wealth, material goods, pleasure, and indulgences in hopes of satisfying this deep need or void within, only to discover that they still feel empty and unfulfilled. Possessions, people, experiences, and religion cannot fill this void.

This void can only be filled by God. He designed it that way so that we would seek after a relationship with Him, which He made available through His Son Jesus' death on the cross and resurrection where Jesus took our unrighteousness and exchanged it for His righteousness. Jesus is the gateway to a meaningful and fulfilling life with God. When we accept Jesus as our Savior and repent of our sins, God fills the void with His presence; He unites Himself to our inner most being. Only the Creator Himself can satisfy the deep longings of the human heart.

Jesus is the gateway for us to experience all that God has in store for us. Jesus said in *Matthew 4:19, "Come follow Me."* He also said in *John 14:6, "I am the Way and the Truth and the Life. No one comes to the Father except through Me."*

Jesus is the only one who can forgive our sins so we can fully embrace the life, gifts, and promises God has for us. It has nothing to do with what we've done, good or bad, but has everything to do with God's free gifts of love, mercy, and grace. *John 3:16* reads, *"For God so loved the world that He gave His one and only Son, that whoever believes in Him should not perish but have eternal life."*

This life is available to everyone; it's ours if we ask for it and commit our lives to Christ Jesus. Have you made a commitment to follow Jesus? Are you ready to follow Jesus now? It's as simple as saying this prayer:

Lord Jesus, for too long I've kept you out of my life. I know I'm a sinner and that I cannot save myself. Forgive my sins and come into my heart, Lord Jesus, and be my Savior. By faith, I receive your love, mercy, grace, forgiveness, and your gift of salvation. I'm ready to trust you as my Lord and Savior. Thank You for dying on the cross bearing my sin, and for rising from the dead on the third day to give me eternal life. I entrust my life to, You. Show me the way. Amen.

2 Corinthians 5:17 (NKJV) says, *"Therefore, if anyone is in Christ, he is a new creation; old things have passed away; behold, all things have become new."*

When Jesus rose from the dead and ascended to Heaven, He said He would not leave us alone but would send the Holy Spirit, the Counselor, to live in our hearts and teach us all things. We are never alone.

RECEIVING JESUS CHRIST AS OUR LORD AND SAVIOR ENABLES US TO:

- Have a relationship with God as a loving parent *(2 Corinthians 6:18)*
- Be newly created or born again; the old is gone *(2 Corinthians 5:17)*

- Accept forgiveness and forgive others *(Colossians 3:13)*
- Have a future full of hope *(John 10:28-30)*
- Have a fulfilling life that no one can steal from us *(John 10:10)*
- Obtain freedom as we are made into the image of the Lord *(2 Corinthians 3:17-18)*
- Experience the reality of 3000+ promises in the Bible *(2 Peter 1:4 NLT)*
- Live a worry-free life *(Matthew 6:25-34)*
- Have a Counselor that will teach us all things *(John 14:26)*
- Have peace and a trouble-free heart *(John 14:27)*
- Have joy *(John 15:11)*
- Have a lifetime of favor *(Psalm 30:5)*
- Experience life in all its fullness *(John 10:10)*

CHAPTER 22

THE TRUTH SETS US FREE

John 1:14   1 Jn 1:1 (handwritten)

YOU WILL KNOW GOD BY KNOWING THE BIBLE *Because* (handwritten)
Jesus is the word made flesh (handwritten)

God uses His Word (the Bible) to teach us how to live a worry-free life of peace and joy while trusting in Him and the promises He has for all believers. The Bible is our guide, a lamp unto our feet, a light to our path, our weapon against the enemy, plus it teaches us to know God's heart and mind in all of life's situations. The Word of God is penned, by God Himself, through people's gifting. Reading the Bible is the most important activity we can do on a daily basis. Life works much better when we follow the instructions of our Creator. We can have a close relationship with God. It's comforting to know that when we draw near to God, He draws near to us *(James 4:8)*. He doesn't force the relationship because God is a gentleman who would rather we come to Him because we want to.

DOES YOUR MIND NEED TO BE RENOVATED?

The Bible says in *Romans 12:2-3 (NKJV), "And do not be conformed to this world, but be transformed by the renewing of your mind, that you may prove what is that good, and acceptable, and perfect will of God."* We should not allow worldly fads *to* pressure us in such a way that we become like the world and conform to its ways; acting, thinking, or saying something that is not representative of who we are in Jesus Christ. Instead, we should be transformed

170

by the renewing of our mind, to be like Christ.

Renewing means "Renovation." The replacement of what was formerly present in our mind with something better. Tear out the old that does not fit and replace it with new thoughts and plans that align with God's will for our lives.

How is that renewing going to take place?

Rom 10:14 -17

The Word of God is taken in by listening to sermons or reading or studying; hopefully by reading the Bible every day. The Spirit of God then takes the Word that has been ingested into our system; and He uses it to show us the things in our life that shouldn't be there. Little by little, there is a replacement of the old things with the new things. The Holy Spirit and the Word of God work in unison with each other, to convict us and cause us to be renewed and changed from the inside out. By renewing our minds in the Word of God, we learn God's good, acceptable and perfect will for our lives. *"good", then "acceptable", then finally "perfect"*

The transformation God does in us is not something that happens all at once – it's a continuous process. As we read and study God's Word, we become more and more what God has called us to be. *Ro 10:17 The disciples studied the living word and became like him. Jn 6:68 Acts 5:42*

2 Corinthians 4:16 (NKJV), reads, *"Therefore we do not lose heart. Even though our outward man is perishing, yet the inward man is being renewed day by day."* The Christian life is a day by day renewal. *Acts 5:42* It's a reprogramming of our mind to be more like the mind of God, while we live and do His will. It's an on-going process that we as believers should welcome. The Word of God is the truth that will set us free.

Take time to read, reflect, and meditate on the following scriptures about the Word of God:

"Jesus replied: 'Your mistake is that you don't know the Scriptures, and you don't know the power of God.'" (Matthew 22:29 NLT)

"And be renewed in the spirit of your mind." (Ephesians 4:23 NKJV)

"All Scripture is God-breathed and is useful for teaching, rebuking, correcting and training in righteousness." (2 Timothy 3:16)

"For the Word of God is alive and active. Sharper than any double-edged sword, it penetrates even to dividing soul and spirit, joints and marrow; It judges the thoughts and attitudes of the heart." (Hebrews 4:12)

"Your Word is a lamp to my feet and a light to my path." (Psalm 119:105)

"Then you will know the Truth, and the Truth will set you free." (John 8:32)

make
a strange word

PART XI

THE BELIEVERS ROLE
IN THE CHURCH
is there a role also for unbelievers?

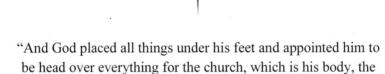

"And God placed all things under his feet and appointed him to be head over everything for the church, which is his body, the fullness of him who fills everything in every way."
Ephesians 1:22-23

CHAPTER 23

---*---

THE Body of CHRIST;
IT TAKES Us All

RELIGION THAT GOD ACCEPTS

"If anyone considers himself religious and yet does not keep a tight rein on his tongue, he deceives himself and his religion is worthless. Religion that God our Father accepts as pure and faultless is this: to look after orphans and widows in their distress and to keep oneself from being polluted by the world."
(James 1:26-27)

BODY OF CHRIST - THE DEFINITION

Each person who believes that Jesus Christ died for their sins is a member of the Body of Christ (the church) and has a specific role to play. *1 Corinthians 12:27* says, *"Now you are the Body of Christ, and each one of you is a part of it."*

Every believer is called to use their gifts to help the church carry out its purpose in the world. Believers offer to serve out of devotion and love for Christ, and the sacrifice He made on the cross that secured for them eternal life in heaven.

Mature Christians are to guide new believers in finding their gifting and learning how to use their gifts wisely. New believers should listen to God's voice closely before they venture out to use their gifts in the church. *Proverbs 1:5* states, *"Let the wise listen and add to their learning, and let the discerning get guidance."* Titus 2 says that the older (mature believers), should teach the younger (new believers). Gifts are not an afterthought, but God's plan to shape us and prepare us for our role in the building of His Kingdom.

The first Biblical reference to the body was made during the last supper that Jesus had with his disciples. *Mark 14:22,* reads, *"While they were eating, Jesus took bread, gave thanks and broke it, and gave it to his disciples, saying, 'Take it; this is my body."* 1 Corinthians 11:26 reads, *"For whenever you eat this bread and drink this cup, you proclaim the Lord's death until He comes."* This symbolic act was the beginning of the communion service where the Body of Believers acknowledges Jesus' death on the cross for them and His resurrection.

BODY OF CHRIST - THE UNIT

There is a plan for how things should function in the Body of Christ. Jesus is the Head, as described in *Ephesians 1:22-23, "And God placed all things under His feet and appointed Him to be Head over everything for the church, which is His body, the fullness of Him who fills everything in every way."*

Like all bodies, the Body of Christ has many parts, and each believer is an equal part of the Body. No one is better, or more favored than anyone else; to think so is prideful. The body consists of many parts, limbs, organs, bones, etc., and functions best with all the parts intact. The diversity of gifts, each supporting the other, gives strength and vitality to the Body. Each believer is a functioning part of the Body as described in *1 Corinthians 12:12-27 NLT* below:

"The human body has many parts, but the many parts make up one whole body. So it is with the body of Christ. Some of us are Jews, some are Gentiles, some are slaves, and some are free. But we have all been baptized into one body by one Spirit, and we all share the same Spirit.

Yes, the body has many different parts, not just one part. If the foot says, "I am not a part of the body because I am not a hand," that does not make it any less a part of the body. And if the ear says, "I am not part of the body because I am not an eye," would that make it any less a part of the body? If the whole body were an eye, how would you hear? Or if your whole body were an ear, how would you smell anything?

But our bodies have many parts, and God has put each part just where he wants it. How strange a body would be if it had only one part! Yes, there are many parts, but only one body. The eye can never say to the hand, "I don't need you." The head can't say to the feet, "I don't need you."

In fact, some parts of the body that seem weakest and least important are actually the most necessary. And the parts we regard as less honorable are those we clothe with the greatest care. So we carefully protect those parts that should not be seen, while the more honorable parts do not require this special care. So God has put the body together such that extra honor and care are given to those parts that have less dignity. This makes for harmony among the members, so that all the members care for each other. If one part suffers, all the parts suffer with it, and if one part is honored, all the parts are glad.

All of you together are Christ's body, and each of you is a part of it."

We can see when we read the above passage, there is no hierarchy in the Body, the gift of being a pastor is not more important than the person with the gift of helps, the gift of prophecy is not more important than the gift of encouragement, etc. Each member of the Body of Believers is equally valuable in God's eyes. As believers, we need one another in order to function as a whole.

BODY OF CHRIST – PERSONAL APPLICATION

As a part of the church, how can we serve and help to improve the Body of Christ? The Body is to be respected and treated with honor, care, and holiness, as it is a holy entity. According to *Matthew 28:19,* the only job description the church has is to make disciples and we accomplish that by working together using our gifts. Discipleship does not promise a life of ease,

176

nor is it a journey of faith. It is about denying oneself to put the purposes of Jesus Christ first, letting Him be our resource for strength and direction, which results in a meaningful and fulfilling life.

What we must realize is that God will work in and through any believer who is willing to let Him. We don't need special schooling or qualifications, Jesus demonstrated this when He chose His disciples who were unschooled fishermen with no formal religious training. In *1 Corinthians 2:3-5,* Paul says, *"I came to you in weakness and fear, and with much trembling. My message and my preaching were not with wise and persuasive words, but with a demonstration of the Spirit's power, so that your faith might not rest on men's wisdom, but on God's power."* The disciples relied on God's power and wisdom, not their own, and God wants us to do the same. Gifts are sacred, and every person should pray when they feel inspired to use their gift to ensure it is the Holy Spirit's prompting and not their own.

The evil all around us is evidence that Christians need to get back to a life where we surrender to Almighty God's Will instead of our own. Let's start asking God to use us. He wants us to be His voice, eyes, ears, hands, and feet on earth. He wants us to help shed light on the darkness that surrounds us. Our gifts will come to life when we turn our heart toward God and seek to live as a disciple of Jesus Christ. *Proverbs 3:5-6* says, *"Trust in the Lord with all your heart and lean not on your own understanding; in all your ways submit to Him, and He will make your paths straight."*

The Bible provides several action steps for building up the Body of Christ. As believers in Jesus Christ we are called to:

Promote Truth and Unity

The truth is the gospel message. Obedience to Christ and the truth represented in God's Holy Word are necessary for every believer. We, therefore, need to know what the Bible says by reading it, meditating on it, and asking God to reveal it to us.

God wants us to live a Holy life, separate from the world. *Romans 12:1-2* reads,

"Therefore, I urge you, brothers and sisters, in view of God's mercy, to offer your bodies as a living sacrifice, holy and pleasing to God—this is your true and proper worship. Do not conform to the pattern of this world but be transformed by the renewing of your mind. Then you will be able to test and approve what God's will is, His good, pleasing and perfect will."

Unless we are totally surrendered to God, we will never be effective in carrying out His will in our lives. God has a plan and a purpose for each and every one of us. We must die to self so He can live through us. It is in the surrendering of our lives to the Lord Jesus that He moves to reveal His gifting, will, and ministry to us. James 1:8

Take time to read, reflect, and meditate on the following scriptures about truth and unity:

"Therefore, each of you must put off falsehood and speak truthfully to his neighbor, for we are all members of one body." (Ephesians 4:25)

"Then you will know the Truth, and the Truth will set you free." (John 8:32)

Jesus said, "I am the Way and the Truth and the Life. No one comes to the Father except through Me." (John 14:6)

"We demolish arguments and every pretension that sets itself up against the knowledge of God, and we take captive every thought to make it obedient to Christ." (2 Corinthians 10:5)

SERVE GOD USING YOUR GIFTS

1 Sam 19:24

No matter what gift(s) a person has, each gift is given by the Holy Spirit. The Holy Spirit decides which gifts each one of us should have. We are responsible to use and sharpen our gifts, but we can take no credit for what God has freely given us.

When we use one of our gifts, we witness how things are done in the Kingdom of Heaven. The Lord shares His gifts with us so that He can show His love and redemptive power to the world.

178

No matter what our age, we have a magnificent destiny that is far beyond our human needs and limitations. Let's allow God to flow through the gifts He has bestowed on us to spread His love and redemptive power to this broken world. Doing so results in a blessed and fulfilled life where the dash on our tombstone between the day we were born and the day we die has significant meaning in God's Kingdom because what God wanted to accomplish on earth, He did through us.

In *Matthew 5:16* Jesus said, *"Let your light shine before men, that they may see your good deeds and praise your Father in heaven."* When we use our gifts as He directs, to help others, they will see Jesus in us and praise Him for the help they have received. Rom 14:11 even his enemies

When church members work together doing the work God intended, the church will be healthy and will function as it was designed to, with miracles and wonders, making it a light that illuminates the darkness in the world.

Are you living your life for Jesus Christ or are you too busy doing things that have no eternal value?

Take time to read, reflect, and meditate on the following scriptures:

"For we are His workmanship, created in Christ Jesus for good works, which God prepared beforehand, that we should walk in them." (Ephesians 2:10 ESV)

"We are therefore Christ's ambassadors, as though God were making His appeal through us." (2 Corinthians 5:20)

PRACTICE RIGHT LIVING

Negative thoughts about ourselves or anyone else disappear when we focus on forgiving serving and loving others. When we direct our energy to obey God and use our gifts to serve; the result is personal peace, joy, and fulfillment that we wouldn't otherwise have known.

Our righteousness must:

- Come from what God does in us, not what we do by ourselves
- Be God-centered, not self-centered
- Be based on reverence for God, not approval from people
- Go beyond keeping the law to accepting and living a life based on God's mercy and grace through Jesus Christ

Take time to read, reflect, and meditate on the following scriptures about right living:

"I am not ashamed of the gospel, because it is the power of God for the salvation of everyone who believes..." (Romans 1:16)

"For the grace of God that brings salvation has appeared to all men. It teaches us to say "No" to ungodliness and worldly passions and to live self-controlled, upright and godly lives in this present age." (Titus 2:11-12)

"His divine power has given us everything we need for life and godliness through our knowledge of Him who called us by His own glory and goodness. Through these, He has given us His very great and precious promises, so that through them you may participate in the divine nature and escape the corruption in the world caused by evil desires. For this very reason, make every effort to add to your faith goodness; and to goodness, knowledge; and to knowledge, self-control; and to self-control, perseverance; and to perseverance, godliness; and to godliness, brotherly kindness; and to brotherly kindness, love. For if you possess these qualities in increasing measure, they will keep you from being ineffective and unproductive in your knowledge of our Lord Jesus Christ." (2 Peter 1:3-8)

Share Your Story and Testimony of How You Came to Believe in Jesus

Today most Christians feel like they are of little value to God and therefore make no effort to affect the world around them. When we live for Christ and do His will, our lives glow like lights showing others what Christ is like. Sharing our story or testimony is very powerful and displays God's transformational miracle-working power. Therefore, be bold sharing your story, using your voice, and being faithful to your calling.

We hide our lights by:

- Not speaking when we feel prompted by the Holy Spirit to speak
- Accepting and going along with the crowd
- Denying the light
- Allowing sin to dim our light
- Not explaining our light and the love of God to others
- Ignoring the needs of others
- Allowing Satan to convince us that we are of little value to God

Be a beacon of truth – don't hide your light from the rest of the world. Your light exposes darkness, and that is your primary job as a Christian. Jesus teaches about light in *Matthew 5:14-16, "You are the light of the world. A city on a hill cannot be hidden. Neither do people light a lamp and put it under a bowl. Instead they put it on its stand, and it gives light to everyone in the house. In the same way, let your light shine before men, that they may see your good deeds and praise your Father in heaven."*

Worship

God delights in our admiration for Him through praise and worship. Reflect on the following scriptures about praising our Lord:

"It is good to praise the LORD and make music to Your name, O Most High, to proclaim Your love in the morning and Your faithfulness at night." (Psalm 92:1-2)

"Give thanks to the Lord, for He is good; His love endures forever." (1 Chronicles 16:34)

"Praise the Lord, O my soul; all my inmost being, praise His holy name."
(Psalm 103:1)

Love One Another

To love one another well, we need to understand the four personality styles that God created and their gifts, needs, joys, values, and stressors. This helps us be more accepting and less critical of our differences. Having a close walk with Christ makes keeping what Jesus referred to as the most important commandments, loving the Lord your God and loving our neighbor, much easier.

Take time to read, reflect, and meditate on the following scriptures about loving one another:

"Dear friends, since God so loved us, we also ought to love one another." *(1 John 4:11)*

"The whole Body, joined and held together by every supporting ligament, grows and builds itself up in love, as each part does its work." *(Ephesians 4:16)*

"Above all, love each other deeply, because love covers over a multitude of sins." *(1 Peter 4:8)*

PART XII

Reflection

"For we are God's workmanship, created in Christ Jesus to
do good works, which God prepared in advance for us to do."
Ephesians 2:10

Chapter 24

---✦---

To God Be the Glory

IT'S NOT WHAT WE HAVE, BUT WHAT GOD HAS THAT FLOWS THROUGH US

Doing great things isn't dependent on our abilities but on God's miracle-working power. We are not called to do things outside of our spiritual gifting and therefore don't need to force ourselves to do things that are meant for others to do. Our primary responsibility is to make ourselves available by being God's conduit for the work He desires to do. He will perform the necessary miracle, and we need to make sure He gets the praise, honor, and glory!

Acts 3:1-7 is an example of how God flows through us. Peter and John were on their way to the temple when a crippled beggar asked them for money. Peter said in *verse 6, "Silver and gold I do not have, but what I have I give you. In the name of Jesus Christ of Nazareth, walk."* The beggar's healing was instant, and he began to walk.

Let us be worthy of the calling that God has on our lives by living a surrendered life. *"That our God may count you worthy of His calling, and that by His power He may fulfill every good purpose of yours and every act prompted by your faith. We pray this so that the name of our Lord Jesus may be glorified in you, and you in Him, according to the grace of our God and the Lord Jesus Christ."* *(2 Thessalonians 1:11-12)*

It's not what we have, but what God has that flows through us. We have to be bold like the disciples were. God presents the opportunities, and our job is to be obedient and use the gifts we have been given in Jesus' name.

The same power that raised Jesus from the dead lives in every born-again believer. It's the power of Jesus Christ that causes change, transformation, and miracles to happen. I encourage you to step out in faith, as Peter did in *Matthew 14:29* when he walked on water; expecting the miraculous, by trusting in Jesus who is faithful.

Take time to read, reflect, and meditate on the following scriptures about giving glory to God who deserves our thanksgiving, praise, and worship and the boldly use your gifts to bless the Body and further His Kingdom, in Jesus' name.

"The Son radiates God's own glory and expresses the very character of God, and He sustains everything by the mighty power of His command." (Hebrews 1:3)

"For from Him and through Him and to Him are all things. To Him be the glory forever!" (Romans 11:36)

"Glory to God in the highest heaven, and on earth peace to those on whom His favor rests." (Luke 2:14)

"And my God will meet all your needs according to the riches of His glory in Christ Jesus. To our God and Father be glory for ever and ever. Amen." (Philippians 4:19-20)

"Now all glory to God, who is able, through His mighty power at work within us, to accomplish infinitely more than we might ask or think." (Ephesians 3:20 NLT)

CHAPTER 25

GOD HAS CREATED ME
UNIQUELY GIFTED FOR A REASON

Take time to outline and reflect on the way God specially designed you and what He has planned for your life.

- I am an: Extrovert/Introvert (Covered in chapter 5)

  Add a check mark next to how you best restore your energy below:

  My energy is restored when I am;

  1. _____ with people, or
  2. _____ alone

- My Personality Style Ranking is: (Covered in chapter 6)

  1. _____Dominant Style

  2. _____Secondary Backup Style

  3. _____Third Style

  4. _____Challenging Style

- My Spiritual Gift Lineup is: (Covered in chapter 12)

    1. _____

    2. _____

    3. _____

    4. _____

    5. _____

- My Purpose Statement is: (Covered in chapter 17 and 18)

_____

_____

_____

_____

_____

- My next step to live out God's calling on my life is:

_____

_____

_____

_____

_____

ABOUT THE AUTHOR

Erika Larsson is passionate about helping people identify their God-given gifts to clarify their purpose. She believes that by serving others we live the life we were created to live; a life of joy, passion, and fulfillment. Erika has a soft spot for anyone who suffers from adversity and loves motivating people to use their inherent gifts to make a difference in their community. If everyone does a little, a lot of needs can quickly be eliminated.

For 25-years, Erika has been a personality-style enthusiast. She attributes her personal and professional success to understanding the four personality temperaments that we interact with in our day-to-day activities.

Erika brings energy and enthusiasm to her writing and speaking. She is a spirited trainer who encourages people to be authentic while maximizing their potential and living out loud. She has given creative workshops since 1990 and has spoken to audiences as large as 3,000.

Her goal is to challenge, inspire and motivate people to use their natural gifts; creating lasting relationships based on total acceptance and mutual respect. Her mission is to share her knowledge and expertise with people who want to make a difference in the world by using their spiritual gifts to be God's hands and feet.

You can find information about Erika's training seminars, speaking, video blog, and books at:

www.ErikaLarsson.com

SEMINARS AND TESTIMONIALS

If you desire a deeper understanding of yourself, your spiritual gifting, and your God-given purpose, you can host or attend Erika's Rising Higher seminar by contacting her at:

www.ErikaLarsson.com
admin@ErikaLarsson.com

Rising Higher - Seminar Testimonials:

"I went to the workshop for fun and to gain pointers that I could use in business. Erika's teaching delivered more than expected; it was so practical that I use what I learned on a daily basis. Her teaching helped me gain a deeper understanding of myself and the behavioral traits of the different personality types, resulting in better relationships with my family, coworkers, and spouse. I'm able to appreciate our differences and can see the contribution that each one brings to my world. By understanding the people that I interact with, I'm better able to navigate through life without all the speedbumps."
~ *L. Wise, CFO of Cement Distributors Inc.*

"I was really excited to attend this seminar. Wow! It was amazing! Life changing for sure. Can't wait to see what God has for me to use his gifts."
~ *K. Thompson, Loan Officer - Prime Lending*

"Erika helped me clarify my gifts. I've been able to use the information I learned to launch myself out of "stuck mode." My new level of clarity helps me to see myself and others in a positive light, giving me a newfound boldness to use my gifts to live the life I was created to live. Erika's encouragement will inspire you to become all that God meant for you to be. I owe some of my most recent success to the wisdom I've gained from Erika's teachings."
~ *J. Hylton, Wellness Advocate*

"Every person deserves to understand the gifts that God has freely given each and every one of us. Don't let those gifts sit on a shelf un-used and un-enjoyed. By learning our own gifts, we are set free to acknowledge and celebrate those gifts in others."
~ *K. Stuard, Health, and Lifestyle Coach*

"I was tired of trying to serve as I saw others serving in the world around me. Erika's teachings helped me to realize that I did not need to mimic other people's serving styles. I learned that I'm uniquely created with specific gifts that line up with the purpose God has designed for me. Understanding my spiritual gifts and personality traits, and that of others has allowed me to embrace my God-given calling and purpose joyfully."

~ *C. Weier, Founder, and CEO of WISE Women/Women Inspiring Successful Entrepreneurs*

"Erika is passionate about this topic and is truly inspiring in sharing a much-needed seminar on gifting and purpose."

~ *D. L. Thomsen, Healthy Lifestyle Coach*

"When I attended Erika's workshop, covering the content of this book, I had three breakthrough realizations. First, there are many people in their forties and later, who still do not know themselves in vital ways (I found out that I was not alone). Second, this can be for many reasons, including: how we were raised, effects of our life experiences and/or unknowingly living to "please others" vs. being who God wired us to be. Finally, Erika's teaching inspired me to reflect on who I am, in ways I had not yet done. Through this, I saw how I can best use my authentic, God-given gifts.

We are all uniquely wired in beautiful and meaningful ways. I recommend attending Erika's workshop and reading this book, as your next steps, to opening endless possibilities for both knowing yourself better and blessing those you love, serve and influence in wonderful ways that only you can."

~ *K. Sciarrotta, Continuous Improvement Practitioner*

"Understanding my personality style and spiritual gifts and that of others is more helpful than most realize. This helps us rejoice where we are and move where we are to move."

~ *J. Hook, Retired teacher and missionary*

"This is my first workshop, and Erika's sharing and teaching helped me so much. I have taken away the boldness to live in faith and peace for my new career. Erika's energy is comforting, relaxed and professional. The workshop is a place to feel ok to share personal experiences."

~ *K. Segner*

ERIKA'S BOOKS:

Erika's books can be ordered on Amazon.com, www.ErikaLarsson.com or emailing admin@ErikaLarsson.com

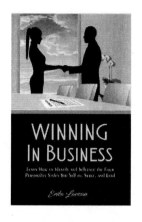

WINNING IN BUSINESS - Learn How to Identify and Influence the Four Personality Styles You Sell To, Serve, and Lead ($20.00 + shipping and handling)

"If you are looking to understand how to serve your customers at an even higher level in ways you likely have never considered, get Erika's book, *WINNING IN BUSINESS - Learn How to Identify and Influence the Four Personality Styles You Sell To, Serve, and Lead*. It offers insights from a potent personality perspective that helps you earn credibility, build trust, and establish loyal business relationships. Erika offers her expertise and observations from over 25 years of experience in the field of customer service with her easy-to-read, straightforward, spirited writing style. You'll learn about yourself, your colleagues, and your competition as well as your customers in this valuable book."

Mary Miscisin, Author of Personality Lingo and Showing Our True Colors, Noted Speaker

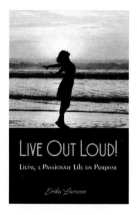

LIVE OUT LOUD! Living a Passionate Life on Purpose ($20.00 + shipping and handling)

"One of the greatest blessings of being human is the opportunity we have of being in relationship with others. It is also one of the greatest challenges, whether in a business or personal context. I have helped others work on their relationships. I've also had to work on my own over the years and continue to do so. Erika's book, *LIVE OUT LOUD! Living a Passionate Life on Purpose,* is a welcome addition to the literature available on relationships. It gave my wife and me helpful information and a greater understanding of ourselves and each other. I heartily recommend it to you."

Keith Hook, Mission Leader/Former Missionary and Pastor

REFERENCES

Erika Larsson
©2017 *Winning in Business*
Kindle Direct Publishing, North Charleston, South Carolina

Mary Miscisin
©2014 *Personality Lingo*
CreateSpace Independent Publishing Platform, North Charleston, South
Carolina

Roderick L. Evans
©2014 *The Spiritual Gifts*
Abundant Truth Publishing, Camden, North Carolina

Kay Arthur, David & BJ Lawson - Precept Ministries Int.
©2010 *Understanding Spiritual Gifts*
WaterBrook Press, Colorado Springs, Colorado

Don & Katie Fortune
©2009 *Discover Your God-Given Gifts*
Chosen Books, Grand Rapids, Michigan

Discovering Your Spiritual Gift DNA Scoresheet

Mark your answer next to each bold question number by circling the number that appropriately describes your answer for each question as follows:

0 = NEVER   1 = SELDOM   2 = OFTEN   3 = ALWAYS

#	N	S	O	A	#	N	S	O	A	#	N	S	O	A	Total	Gift Name
1	0	1	2	3	25	0	1	2	3	49	0	1	2	3	1.	
2	0	1	2	3	26	0	1	2	3	50	0	1	2	3	2.	
3	0	1	2	3	27	0	1	2	3	51	0	1	2	3	3.	
4	0	1	2	3	28	0	1	2	3	52	0	1	2	3	4.	
5	0	1	2	3	29	0	1	2	3	53	0	1	2	3	5.	
6	0	1	2	3	30	0	1	2	3	54	0	1	2	3	6.	
7	0	1	2	3	31	0	1	2	3	55	0	1	2	3	7.	
8	0	1	2	3	32	0	1	2	3	56	0	1	2	3	8.	
9	0	1	2	3	33	0	1	2	3	57	0	1	2	3	9.	
10	0	1	2	3	34	0	1	2	3	58	0	1	2	3	10.	
11	0	1	2	3	35	0	1	2	3	59	0	1	2	3	11.	
12	0	1	2	3	36	0	1	2	3	60	0	1	2	3	12.	
13	0	1	2	3	37	0	1	2	3	61	0	1	2	3	13.	
14	0	1	2	3	38	0	1	2	3	62	0	1	2	3	14.	
15	0	1	2	3	39	0	1	2	3	63	0	1	2	3	15.	
16	0	1	2	3	40	0	1	2	3	64	0	1	2	3	16.	
17	0	1	2	3	41	0	1	2	3	65	0	1	2	3	17.	
18	0	1	2	3	42	0	1	2	3	66	0	1	2	3	18.	
19	0	1	2	3	43	0	1	2	3	67	0	1	2	3	19.	
20	0	1	2	3	44	0	1	2	3	68	0	1	2	3	20.	
21	0	1	2	3	45	0	1	2	3	69	0	1	2	3	21.	
22	0	1	2	3	46	0	1	2	3	70	0	1	2	3	22.	
23	0	1	2	3	47	0	1	2	3	71	0	1	2	3	23.	
24	0	1	2	3	48	0	1	2	3	72	0	1	2	3	24.	